Zapp!

IN EDUCATION

IN EDUCATION

HOW EMPOWERMENT CAN IMPROVE THE QUALITY OF INSTRUCTION, AND STUDENT AND TEACHER SATISFACTION

WILLIAM C. BYHAM, PH.D.,
WITH JEFF COX AND
KATHY HARPER SHOMO

FAWCETT COLUMBINE • NEW YORK

All characters, schools, and events portrayed in this book are
fictitious; and any resemblance to actual people, sites, or events
is purely coincidental.

A Fawcett Columbine Book
Published by Ballantine Books

This edition published by arrangement with Development
Dimensions International Publications.

Library of Congress Catalog Card Number: 92-90653

ISBN: 0-449-90796-1

Manufactured in the United States of America

First Edition: August 1992

10 9 8 7 6 5 4 3 2 1

To my mother, Brice Byham,
who for 17 years Zapped
junior high school English students in
Parkersburg, West Virginia. I hope that this
book can help other educators have a positive
impact on as many lives.

Bill Byham

PREFACE

Why Should You Read This Book?

That's a fair question. Why should a serious, rational adult take time to read a fable about problems and achievements of teachers, administrators, and students in a make-believe school that is headed by a guy named Joe Mode?

One reason is the need to improve the quality and efficiency of American education. America cannot remain a competitive economic leader unless we effect major changes in our educational system. We must do a better job of preparing individuals who can succeed and enjoy working in a highly competitive, ever-changing environment. It is an awesome responsibility!

Educators have been looking for quick fixes for two hundred years—with little success. No new technology or teaching method has catapulted American education to new heights. The thesis of this book is that the solution to America's education challenge lies in individual schools that develop an ethic of continuous improvement among staff, teachers, and students. If, on a daily basis, all these groups keep looking for better ways—regardless of how small the individual improvements—the accumulation of these actions will lead to the improved education that we all seek.

Not surprisingly, continuous improvement is a difficult concept to implant. Why should individuals put in extra effort to try out new ideas, to help students with particular difficulties, to reduce the amount of paperwork, or to take on difficult learning challenges? All these activities require extra time and effort, and we have plenty to do already. The answer is the pride and sense of accomplishment that come from owning a job and feeling responsible for its outcome—*empowerment*.

Improved education is a destination, and continuous improvement is the road to that destination—a never-ending road. Empowerment is the engine that moves people along on this road. People are motivated to make continuous improvements because they enjoy the sense of pride they obtain from their accomplishments.

A second reason for reading this book is that empowerment improves the quality of life for individuals. Empowered people see themselves as meaningful, contributing individuals who are respected for their ideas and contributions. They are involved and committed to their activities, and they gain satisfaction from the success of those activities. For empowered individuals, work and learning are interesting, challenging, and rewarding. The school day goes by quickly for empowered people because they are committed and interested in their activities.

We agree with John Dewey, the father of democratic education, who was asked near the end of his life what he had learned during his career. He answered, "What I have learned is that the purpose of education is to allow each individual to come into full possession of his or her personal power." Thus, one of the goals of American education is to start students on a road toward the feelings of success and achievement that come from commitment, ownership, and responsibility for their own educational progress. We must prepare students to achieve and develop the self-confidence needed to handle the hurdles they will encounter in their lives beyond the classroom.

Importantly, teachers need to have the skills to empower. But before teachers can empower their students, teachers themselves must be empowered. That is the main thrust of this book. It is designed to help administrators and teachers understand on a fundamental level what empowerment really is, why it is important, and how its principles can be used in schools everywhere.

Zapp! in Education is an adaptation of *Zapp! The Lightning of Empowerment,* which focuses on life in a corporate setting. Because of the original book's tremendous success—and the great interest in it shown by educators—we decided to develop a variation of the story to show how the same concepts can be used in schools. Our hope is that you will find *Zapp! in Education* as helpful to you as managers and employees in business tell us the original *Zapp!* is to them.

Why did we write the book in the style of a fable? Because even the best ideas are of small value unless communicated well. *Zapp! in Education* is written the way it is so that we can take an abstract concept and help you visualize it in action—in lively but meaningful terms. We want the book to be easy to understand, yet challenging to the imagination. Fable or not, this is a realistic, practical book. After you have read this book, you will have the knowledge to begin using its underlying ideas, as well as the basis for beginning formal training in empowerment skills. So enjoy *Zapp! in Education*. And, most important, learn about a concept that is vital to personal and professional success.

William C. Byham
Pittsburgh, Pennsylvania

PART I

Situation Normal

I

Once upon a time, in a magic land called America, there lived a normal guy named Ralph Rosco.

Ralph taught in Normal Middle School in Normalburg, USA. For years, Normal School had been a good school that had gained the respect of the community it served. Many of the town's leading citizens had been educated there, and the townspeople had high regard for the school and its staff.

As you might expect, just about everything was normal at Normal, including the understanding of who was normally supposed to do what:

Central Office folks did the thinking.
Principals did the talking.
Teachers did the doing.
And students did whatever they were told to do—
    well, most of the time.

That was the way it had always been—ever since the town's foreparents had built the school—and so everybody just assumed that was the way it should always be.

Ralph was your normal type of teacher. He came to school prepared. He enjoyed working with his students. He handled the extracurricular assignments his principal asked him to do. And at the end of the day, he dragged himself home to get ready to do it all again.

When friends or family asked how he liked teaching, Ralph would say, "Oh, it's all right, I guess. Not very exciting, but I guess that's normal. Anyway, it's a job and the pay is OK."

In truth, teaching at Normal was not very satisfying for Ralph, although he was not sure why. The pay was not the best, but it wasn't bad. The benefits were fine. The other teachers were nice, and the students were usually well behaved. Being off all summer was great. Yet, something seemed to be missing.

But Ralph figured there wasn't much he could do to change things at the school. After all, he reasoned, who would even bother to listen? So he kept his thoughts to himself, and just did what he was told.

Ralph taught science, and his department colleagues were professional and cooperative. They were all considered to be good teachers, although no one really knew what that meant.

One day, on his way back to the classroom from lunch, Ralph happened to be thinking about one of his students and . . . well, he was simply *Zapped* by an idea so original and so full of promise that his head nearly exploded with excitement.

"Wowee! Zowee!! Yeah!!!" exclaimed Ralph, to the shock of all the Normal teachers around him.

In his excitement, Ralph totally forgot that probably nobody would listen, and he ran down the hall to explain his idea to his principal, Joe Mode.

Ralph found Joe busy, doing what he normally did. He was telling everybody what to do as he worried about four pressing student problems he had to deal with, tickets for tomorrow's ballgame, and the PTA meeting that evening. As Joe was scribbling a memo to his staff, he received an urgent call from the Central Office.

Joe's boss, Mary Ellen Krabofski, the assistant superintendent, was quite upset. That morning she had had to deal with a problem at Typical High School. In an advanced English class studying American literature, a boy was to give a report on Mark Twain's *Huckleberry Finn*. The student, who was the son of the town's mortician, had asked his father to bring a casket to school. Inside the casket was a mannequin dressed in a top hat, white gloves, and cane—just like the funeral scene in *Huckleberry Finn*. The student's father even had a hearse waiting outside in the school parking lot.

Because the principal at Typical High School wasn't sure how to deal with the situation, it had become Mary Ellen's problem. This had upset her and put her in a bad mood for the entire day. And just now, a parent had called her to complain about the poor grades one of Joe's teachers had given her son. That's when Mary Ellen decided to call Joe.

"Joe, I want you to start cracking the whip over there," Mary Ellen told him. "Our test scores are just above the fiftieth percentile, and student and teacher apathy is evident in your school. Just this week, I've received three letters from unhappy parents. And now this phone call."

"But I do crack the whip," Joe responded. "Every chance I get."

"Well," said Mary Ellen, "whatever you're doing, it isn't good enough. The superintendent wants all of us to do better. He says that funding is short, and it's getting shorter. Test scores are low, and they're getting lower. Parent and student complaints are numerous, and they're getting more numerous. So you'd better do something fast—or else!"

"But what can I do?" Joe asked in desperation.

"Raise the test scores, Joe! Improve school morale! Find ways to save money! Work on community relations! And, above all, do a good job!"

"Right. Got it," said Joe.

"Then get to it!"

They both hung up. That was when Joe saw Ralph standing off to the side, eagerly waiting to talk about his idea.

"So talk," Joe sighed.

As Ralph explained his idea, which was so original and full of promise, Joe continued doing everything he was already doing.

"But that isn't what we discussed at our last faculty meeting," said Joe. "How are you coming with the eighth-grade science projects you're supposed to have judged by the end of the day?"

"OK, I'll finish the projects. But what about my idea?" asked Ralph, still excited.

"It doesn't sound to me like the normal way to do things," said Joe. "And besides, don't you think that if the idea was *really* good, the Central Office would have thought of it?"

At that moment, Ralph was tempted to tell Joe that the Central Office didn't know everything, and that furthermore. . . .

But, being normal, Ralph didn't tell Joe anything. He just nodded and went back to his classroom . . . and Joe went back to telling everybody what to do and worrying about the work that had to be finished before the last bell.

By the end of the day, Ralph somehow had managed not to complete the judging of the eighth-grade science projects. He left them on his desk and bolted for the parking lot with the other teachers. And Joe, with a sense of defeat, sat down at his desk and worried about Mary Ellen Krabofski.

2

One thing to Principal Joe Mode's credit, he was organized. Over the years, he had developed the habit of writing things down, and all this jotting and scribbling had evolved into a notebook he kept at his desk. Joe got out his notebook and wrote down the problem as he saw it.

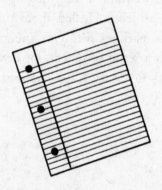

JOE MODE'S NOTEBOOK

The problem as I see it:

- The Central Office wants more . . .
- Because the Board of Education needs more . . .
- Because parents demand more . . .
- Because in order for students to succeed and be happy in life, it takes more . . .

But I can't get my teachers and students to *do* more than the bare minimum.

Then he made a list of all the things he thought might be wrong.

JOE MODE'S NOTEBOOK

What is wrong:

- Hardly anybody gets excited about anything that has to do with teaching or learning.
- The things they do get excited about are outside of school.
- My teachers care about their paychecks, their summers off, and their seniority. Beyond that, forget it.
- The students want to get out of school as fast as possible so they can race home to watch their favorite television shows.
- The general attitude is: Don't do anything you don't have to do. Then do as little as possible.

NOTEBOOK ▥ (cont'd)

- All day, it's like everybody is in slow motion—until it's time to go home. Then it's like watching a videotape in fast forward.
- I talk about doing a better job and what happens? Lots of blank looks.
- Nobody takes any more responsibility than they have to. If the test scores don't go up, it's my problem, not theirs.
- Everybody does just enough to get by so they won't get yelled at or disciplined.
- Nobody cares about improvements; they're all afraid of change. (Me, too, if I'm honest about it.)
- I tell teachers, "If you don't shape up, you'll have a tougher schedule." But all that does is demoralize them, which makes it worse.
- Whenever I try to motivate the teachers or staff members, the results (if any) are short-lived.

Of course, not all of that was absolutely true, and Joe Mode knew there were individual differences among people. But overall, that was how it seemed to him.

Then he started a new page, the page where he would come up with a brilliant solution that would solve the entire problem quickly and easily.

He sat there.

And sat there.

And sat there some more.

But no brilliant solution was forthcoming. Finally, he wrote . . .

JOE MODE'S NOTEBOOK

The solution:

How should I know? I'm just a principal.

What am I going to do now?

- Wait for the Central Office to come up with a brilliant solution.
- Start looking for a new position in case they don't have one.

Why?

Because at the rate things are going, Normal Middle School is going down the tubes—and the educational system of our entire district won't be far behind!

Then he closed his notebook, locked it away in his desk, and headed home. It had not been a good day.

3

Of course, Joe Mode soon forgot about Ralph's idea. But Ralph did not. And, because of that, something very *ab*normal began to take place.

It so happened that Ralph taught in the far end of Corridor B, a place where Principal Joe normally did not venture, because it was out of the way.

This allowed Ralph to take many an open-eyed nap during his planning periods, myopically staring into his planning booklet until he heard footsteps around the corner, when he would snap into his *normal* work pace.

But after he'd come up with his idea, Ralph found he was actually thinking too much to sleep. He would prepare his lesson plans quickly so that he could work on his idea. He started making little sketches. Then he started developing his idea, using equipment from the science lab.

Because no one else would understand, Ralph told no one about what he was doing. He sneaked supplies he needed from other labs, pilfered the trash bins of the industrial arts rooms for scrapped parts he could use, and deviated left and right from standard procedures. He felt he was on a roll to improve education throughout the world.

"This invention is important," thought Ralph. "It's about time somebody really cared about making schools a better place for everyone."

Weeks passed. But, little by little, from the science lab evolved a new piece of educational equipment, one that Ralph called:

The Ralpholator

He worked on it whenever he had the chance . . . planning periods, odd moments, and lunchtime. He began going in earlier and earlier each day so that he would have extra time in the mornings to work on it. He even worked faster on the assignments Principal Joe Mode gave him, finishing most of them quickly so that he would have more time for the Ralpholator.

The other teachers noticed a change in Ralph. He seemed to have more energy. He seemed younger somehow. And his students commented on how much fun it was to be in Ralph's class . . . how he seemed more interested in helping them learn and how often he came up with great ways to illustrate concepts. Ralph and his students seemed *happy*.

Of course, Ralph encountered many setbacks and made a multitude of mistakes. But he stuck with it. He was determined to create something that would help students and teachers everywhere. Finally, one morning when Ralph went in to work early, he was able to solder the last wires into the control panel, and the Ralpholator was finished. Ralph was pleased and proud.

Naturally, Ralph just had to try it out. He connected the wire leads to his chair, sat down, flipped a few switches, and typed a command on his desktop computer.

A high-pitched whine began to emanate from the innards of the strange machine. His work area began to pulsate with an unearthly light. Ralph gripped the arms of his chair, grinned with anticipation—and vanished in a powerful flash.

At the end of the fourth period, Principal Joe needed to know something about a project Ralph was heading, so he asked his assistant principal, Phyllis, to contact Ralph on the intercom. But Ralph was not around.

Grumbling at the inability of the district's personnel director to employ good, reliable teachers these days, Joe stomped toward Corridor B to find Ralph.

After turning left, Joe encountered students being marched toward the exit door by Mr. Hall, another science teacher. Mr. Hall had spent 20 years in the military before entering teaching and, most of the time, behaved in a very regimented way.

"Hup, two, three, four . . . hup, two, three, four!" shouted Mr. Hall at his students.

Joe stepped in front of the group and asked what was going on.

"My classroom is full of smoke. I'm saving the students' lives!" announced Mr. Hall in an excited voice. "The building could burn down, and it's my responsibility to get my students out of here. Move out of the way! Hup, two, three, four . . . hup, two, three, four. . . !"

Joe quickly entered the room and did indeed find some smoke. He identified the smell as a light fixture overheating. Simply turning out the lights solved the problem. He was relieved . . . but what should he do about Mr. Hall and his students?

By this time, other teachers and students had become aware of the happenings and were enjoying the antics of Mr. Hall solving the problem in such a military fashion. Students were laughing and cheering, and the chant, "Hup, two, three, four!" was everywhere.

Running outside, Joe caught up with Mr. Hall and the class.

"Mr. Hall, it's OK now. I've solved the problem," said Joe.

"But what about the fire? What about improving the safety procedures in our school?" shouted Mr. Hall. "I've been here for five years, and nothing has ever been done to solve the safety problems. It wasn't like this in the army."

Joe finally convinced Mr. Hall to re-enter the school with his class, and he called maintenance to repair the fixture. He felt a dull ache across his forehead as he finished solving yet another problem.

Then he remembered Ralph and, for the second time, headed toward Corridor B.

Upon entering Ralph's laboratory, Joe was astounded at the tangle of wires running everywhere.

"What's all this?" he grumbled.

He sat down in Ralph's chair and, in doing so, his elbow hit the return key on the computer keyboard. There was a high-pitched whine, a blinding flash of light, and Joe Mode was transported to the 12th Dimension.

4

Of course, Joe did not know he was in the 12th Dimension. But he knew something had happened. Because, looking around, he saw things were different.

For instance, purple fog was drifting across the floor.

"This is not normal," thought Joe.

And little, crinkly lightning bolts were flitting here and there all around Ralph's laboratory.

"No, this is definitely not normal," thought Joe.

And from the contraption to which all the wires ran, there came a strange pinkish glow.

"This is so *un*-normal, I'm leaving!" thought Joe.

So Joe backed away. He tiptoed through the purple fog, found the exit, and stepped out into the hall, hoping that everything would be normal again. But everything was not. In fact, everything was even more strange.

The fog was thicker and colored in unrelenting shades of gray. Ceilings and corners were shadowy and dark. As Joe was pondering the perplexity of it all, the hall became filled with a ghastly green light. From around the corner came a big, scaly troll. Joe began to back away as the troll stomped toward him. Then he noticed something remarkable. Its claws had fingernail polish.

Fire engine-red fingernail polish. Yes, it was exactly the shade always worn by . . .

Joe looked up into the face of the troll and saw that it was the face of his boss, Mary Ellen Krabofski! She was carrying printouts of some test score reports under one greenish arm, and she walked right past Joe without even seeing him.

Keeping his distance, he followed her through the fog as she headed straight for Joe's office—and straight up to a faint, ice-blue blur, which turned out to be Assistant Principal Phyllis.

"Where's Joe Mode?" asked Mary Ellen, her tail twitching.

Phyllis, whose desk was surrounded by sandbags, dove for cover against the expected incoming barrage.

"Mr. Mode is out," muttered Phyllis.

"Well, when he gets back," said Mary Ellen, as one of the computer printouts she was holding curled up into a large, black ball and sprouted a smoldering fuse, "you give him this."

And she tossed the black ball over the sandbags to Phyllis and left, a pool of ghastly green leaving with her.

Phyllis quickly took the black ball and its sputtering fuse into Joe's office to leave on his desk.

Joe looked around. How dull and gray it was here. "Where are the fluorescent lights?" he wondered. "Why is it so dark?"

All the normal people were here. He saw them working away in the fog, though he did have a little trouble recognizing some of them.

A dim ember in the shadows turned out to be good old Mrs. Estello, there in her normal secretary's chair, pecking away at a computer keyboard—mindlessly making error after error without a break.

"Excuse me," said Joe. "Aren't you going to correct those mistakes?"

But Mrs. Estello's fingers did not even pause.

Peeking into a classroom, Joe saw one of his teachers, Dan, sitting in the dark with both hands tied to the arms of his chair. Dan kept mumbling the same words over and over again—sounding just as monotonous as he always sounded teaching. His voice had no life. His words had no creativity. He was a teacher who might as well have been a robot.

Out in the hall, a whitish form came shuffling out of the fog and emerged as a woman wrapped in mummy tape. The mummy appeared to be Donna, another of Joe's teachers. She seemed to be tied up in administrative knots, as she normally was. Donna was one of those teachers who was usually so busy trying to deal with administrative issues—like sorting party slips or following up on detentions—that she hardly ever had enough time to teach.

"Hey, Donna," called Joe. "What happened here?"

But Donna kept on shuffling by, passing Joe as she went about her work. Her eyes burned like candles as she moved like the living dead.

Just then, a few students walked by. They were also surrounded by thick fog. Their pace was sluggish, and they didn't seem to have any clear direction about where they were going.

What was wrong with everybody? They seemed jailed in dullness, veiled and dim. Joe had to walk right up to them even to see who they were.

And there were walls everywhere. Stone walls, glass walls, steel walls. All the teachers had walls around them, and there were even higher walls around the departments. It was like wandering around in a maze.

"What's happened to everybody? Why doesn't anybody talk to me?!" cried Joe in frustration.

"Because they can't see or hear you," said a voice behind him.

Joe turned around to see Ralph.

"Ralph! What the heck is going on?" asked Joe. "Is this some kind of dream, nightmare, or what?"

"None of the above," Ralph said. "We're both in the 12th Dimension."

And he and Joe sat down while Ralph explained about the Ralpholator.

"Remember when I told you about my new invention?" Ralph asked Joe.

"No," Joe replied. "I guess I wasn't really listening."

"Well," said Ralph, "I was trying to tell you about my Ralpholator. It's this great machine I've invented.

I built it in the lab. It lets us look at teaching and learning in a way that nobody has ever been able to before."

"But why is everything so different here?" Joe asked.

"It's not different," said Ralph. "We're just seeing things we can't see in the normal world."

"Yeah? Like what?"

"Like how people feel about what they're doing . . . what it's like for them on the *inside*," said Ralph.

"Come on! These can't be the people in *my* school," said Joe. "We have only happy teachers and students at Normal School. This is ridiculous. Take me back to the real world."

Normally, Ralph would have been intimidated by Joe Mode and would have kept his mouth shut. But here in the 12th Dimension, where he had discovered far more than his principal, he was emboldened to look Joe in the eye, shake his head, and say, "You just don't get it, do you?"

"Get what?"

"Look around. Joe, this *is* the real world," said Ralph. "It's the same place, but we're seeing it in a different way. That's what the Ralpholator is all about. Did you notice that most of the light around here comes from people?"

"Now that you mention it . . ."

"Take Mrs. Estello. Her light is so dim that it doesn't even make it to her fingertips," said Ralph. "On the other hand, Mary Ellen Krabofski has a lot more, but her light doesn't shine very far beyond herself, does it?"

"So?" asked Joe.

"I think we're seeing an invisible power that people have—invisible in the normal world, but visible in the 12th Dimension," said Ralph.

"Well, that's very interesting," said Joe. "But let's get out of here and go back to work. If the rest of the 12th Dimension is this gloomy, whatever you're talking about isn't worth bothering with."

"But every place isn't like this!" said Ralph. "Some are even darker and gloomier!"

"Oh, terrific."

"But wait—some are brighter, even brilliant. And there is one place you have to see before we go back. I found it as I was walking around."

"Well, I'd love to, but . . ."

"Really, I insist," said Ralph.

So Joe, realizing that Ralph was pretty much in the driver's seat here, said, "OK, show me."

And they went off together through the fog.

5

Ralph had not been missed that morning because a student teacher, Mandy Manley from State Teachers' College, was teaching some of his classes.

Mandy had arrived at school late that day and, because her hair was still in curlers, had hurried to the faculty lounge to make herself presentable before rushing off to her first-period students.

The first class did not go well for Mandy. Sam, a repeater in the class, refused to take his feet off Zack's chair. Henry fell asleep in the back of the room, his loud snores causing laughter throughout the classroom. And in the second period, Andrea cried because her boyfriend, Marcus, was angry with her.

The rest of the morning classes didn't go any better for Mandy. Philip didn't want to be in class at all. He felt embarrassed that he couldn't read as well as the other students, and he had trouble following the experiments in the workbook. Sarah, a slow learner, had trouble paying attention because her mind kept wandering to other things. And Rosa, the brightest student of all, made it clear to everyone that she was bored with everything.

By lunch, Mandy felt she was carrying the world's problems on her shoulders. She was praying that she would get through the day, when Sophie and Benjamin began asking her questions about the upcoming science fair. Deciding that she had enough to handle, Miss Manley sent the two students to the lab to see her supervising teacher, Mr. Rosco.

Sophie was a very good student and a high achiever. She cared about her grades and always aimed to please her teachers. She was highly motivated and well behaved. Benjamin, on the other hand, wasn't motivated or high achieving. Bart Simpson was his idol. None of the teachers knew how to improve Benjamin's grades, even though he had a high IQ and had scored well on standardized tests.

As Sophie and Benjamin entered the lab, they too were overwhelmed by the jumble of wires and electronic paraphernalia strung all over the room. Sophie decided to return to class, since Mr. Rosco wasn't there, but Benjamin—in his inquisitive way—thought otherwise.

"Come on, Sophie," said Benjamin. "Let's look around."

"I don't think we should, Benjamin. We might get into trouble."

"Mr. Rosco won't mind," Benjamin pleaded.

"Well, all right," said Sophie. "Just as long as we

don't touch anything and we get back to class real soon."

"Sure," said Benjamin, and they started looking around. He persuaded Sophie to sit in Mr. Rosco's chair and then—as could be expected from Benjamin—he pushed a button, and Sophie disappeared in a cloud of mist and smoke.

Benjamin was excited—he liked that! But where had she gone? The only way to find out was to sit in Mr. Rosco's chair himself—and push the button again.

As Benjamin got settled in the chair, his fingers trembled as he realized he was just a little afraid of the unknown. But he pressed the button—and immediately Benjamin found himself standing beside Sophie in the 12th Dimension.

"Benjamin, where are we?" asked Sophie in a nervous voice.

"I don't know, Sophie, but let's find out," Benjamin answered.

As the green smoke in front of them began to dissipate, two male images became visible just a few yards away.

"It's Mr. Rosco and Mr. Mode!" Sophie exclaimed.

"Uh, oh," thought Benjamin. "I'm in trouble now."

Forgetting where they were, Principal Joe turned to the two students and demanded to know what they were doing out of their classrooms.

"Well, it's like this," began Benjamin, lowering his

head. "We were looking for Mr. Rosco in the lab, and I just accidentally pushed a button. . . ." His voice trailed off.

"But where are we?" asked Sophie.

Joe turned to Ralph. "You tell them."

So Ralph told Benjamin and Sophie about his invention—the Ralpholator—and how they were in a place where they could actually see how people think and feel about what they are doing.

"This is great!" exclaimed Benjamin.

Sophie wasn't quite as sure. "I think I like it here," she said. "But when can we go back to Normal?"

Ralph assured both his students, and Principal Joe, that in a matter of time—hoping it would be sooner rather than later—all four of them would return to Normal. But in the meantime, they decided to do some exploring in the 12th Dimension.

6

It seemed to Joe that they had journeyed a great distance, though, in fact, it had not been very far at all. As the fog and mist thinned, they walked out of the gloom into brightness. There, in front of them, was another school building. In some ways, it looked a lot like Normal Middle School. In other ways, it did not.

Joe, Ralph, Sophie, and Benjamin ventured inside. As they looked around, they discovered that they were in a fascinating place. Most astounding were the teachers and students.

The teachers radiated a mysterious energy that lit up the place. Some were brighter than others, but their collective brilliance was like a small, warm sun.

And the students—they were doing lots of different things. Some worked alone. Some worked in groups. Yet the light seemed to join them, flowing from one to another, connecting them all.

Everyone was involved—the students *and* the teachers.

Suddenly Ralph called out, "Look! There she is! Watch that woman over there!"

As he spoke, he pointed to a small, robust woman in a cone-shaped wizard hat who wandered about.

"Why is she so special?" asked Joe.

"You'll see," said Ralph, knowingly.

Just then a door swung open, and a young knight staggered out. The suit of armor he wore was battered and scorched. His helmet plumes were burned to cinders. His sword was chipped and cracked. Through the door, Ralph and Joe could see a dragon behind him, panting fire.

Sophie exclaimed, "Why, that's Mr. Zendo! He was my teacher in third grade!"

The woman in the wizard hat approached the knight. She was talking to him when, suddenly, right in front of them, a bolt of lightning appeared in her hand.

As Benjamin yelled, "Watch out!" the bolt forked and flickered and flashed in the woman's hand.

Then, with a graceful windup, she pitched the lightning straight at Mr. Zendo, as Sophie and Benjamin ducked.

"Zapp!" went the lightning through the air. And right into Mr. Zendo.

Joe and Ralph flinched, fearful that Mr. Zendo would be dead on the floor. But, to the contrary, Mr. Zendo instantly became more alive and glowed brightly.

"Thank goodness," Sophie said, very softly.

One by one, the dents in Mr. Zendo's armor popped out. The scorch marks vanished. New plumes sprouted from his helmet as the charred cinders of the old plumes fell off. His sword became whole again. And he marched back into the room to face the dragon once more.

Thinking out loud, Benjamin said, "I remember last year when our social studies teacher taught us about General MacArthur saying, 'I shall return!' Now Mr. Zendo is returning to battle. That's really cool!"

The door to the room closed behind Mr. Zendo. There were roars and shrieks, clangs of metal, blasts of fire, and all kinds of other noises.

The woman quietly moved on.

She went down to the end of the hallway and opened another door. Outside, a narrow path along a spine of solid rock meandered out to meet the yawning emptiness of a bottomless chasm. Some vast distance across the chasm, the path began again. It zigged and zagged through many barren cliffs to a mountain encrusted with diamonds.

But there was no way to cross the chasm.

The woman in the wizard hat put her hand on her chin. Then she called to about a dozen students in one of the classrooms, and they all assembled beside the doorway.

A huge, new bolt of lightning forked and flickered and flashed in the woman's hand. As the woman began to talk to the students, Zapp! went the lightning, branching out to every child in the group. And each of them glowed brighter than before.

Then the woman left them, and they went through the door together, out to the narrow spine of rock, the glow of the lightning going with them.

They walked outside and looked around, talking among themselves, little flickers of their lightning passing among them. Then they began to work.

Some of them built a fire, while others found some cloth, rope, and other materials. Two of them began weaving a large basket, and two others started cutting the cloth and sewing it together into an enormous sack. The rest of them began knotting the rope to make a big net. And pretty soon, it became clear that they were building a hot-air balloon to fly themselves across the chasm to the diamonds on the other side.

"Well, I'll be . . ." said Joe.

"I thought you'd be impressed," glowed Ralph.

"Say, Ralph, what do you think it all means?"

"I don't know, but they sure have their act together," said Ralph.

Then Benjamin chimed in, "This is all so neat! I want to help too!"

Sophie said nothing. She was too overwhelmed.

As Ralph, Joe, Benjamin, and Sophie re-entered the building, they noticed a radiant glow moving from under the door to one of the rooms. Inside, a group of adults were building a wooden structure. Some appeared to be highly skilled carpenters, while others were helping out with the less-difficult tasks—but they were all working together happily.

Lightning streaked back and forth among them and, with each interchange, the structure itself seemed to glow a little brighter. They all were obviously excited about their tasks. As their excitement grew, the lightning bolts became larger.

"Those people look like they're having a ball!" said Ralph.

Next, Joe and Ralph decided to see what was going on in the office. When they got there, they noticed a secretary answering a phone. Little by little, as she handled the call, she began to glow with lightning. After she hung up the phone, they saw her put two fingers to her lips and blow a shrill whistle.

With a clatter of hooves, a silver horse came prancing over to her. Suddenly the theme song from *The Lone Ranger* began to play. Some of the students recognized it as the "William Tell Overture" by Rossini.

The woman gathered up some papers, climbed up on the silver horse, and took the reins.

"Charge!" she yelled, and rode off, the music fading as it followed her down the hall.

Meanwhile, the noises coming from the dragon lair down the hall had slowly diminished. The door opened again. Out came Mr. Zendo.

His armor was battered again, and his plumes were singed. But this time, the dragon followed him . . . meekly. On a leash. And everyone realized that he had not only fought the dragon, he had tamed it.

7

Ralph Rosco, Joe Mode, Sophie, and Benjamin were fascinated by this incredible sight of human lightning flashing among people and everyone working away at these amazing tasks here in—well, wherever this was.

Meanwhile, back in the real world, Mary Ellen Krabofski, fuming at the inability of the district's personnel director to hire good principals these days, had gone to Normal Middle School to see Principal Mode. She was furiously searching Corridor B for Joe Mode so that she could complain about the most recent monthly attendance report.

She stomped into Ralph's lab and tripped over an extension cord, which yanked the plug out of the wall and sent her reeling headfirst into the Ralpholator.

The room went dim, the Ralpholator went dead, and Mary Ellen Krabofski went limp on the floor.

All of a sudden, Ralph, Joe, Sophie, and Benjamin began to feel peculiar. For a few seconds they were not solid anymore. And, before their eyes, the lightning Zapping among the teachers and students dissolved.

Mr. Zendo's armor became a normal shirt and pants.

The wizard became a rather ordinary-looking woman.

The bottomless chasm became just a plain table around which a group of students were laughing and talking.

And the diamond mountain was nowhere to be seen.

Joe, Ralph, Sophie, and Benjamin found that they had suddenly materialized in the middle of a principal's office. In a panic, they were looking for some place to hide, when the rather ordinary-looking woman turned toward them. Joe recognized her immediately: It was Cindy Marks, the principal of Zenith Elementary School.

Surprised to see Joe and the others bumping into each other as they attempted to get away unnoticed, Cindy said, "Welcome to Zenith Elementary School! May I help you with something?"

"No, thanks," said Joe sheepishly. "We're just visiting some of the other schools in the district. . . ."

"Why didn't you say so?" asked Cindy with a smile. "Come on. I'll give you the 50-cent tour."

She led them down the hall. The teachers they met along the way proudly explained what they were doing in their classrooms. Ralph and Joe looked at each other, thinking the same thing: Normal teachers didn't get this excited. In fact, a lot of times they seemed bored.

Nobody seemed to be bored here. Although it looked like any other school, there was something different in the air. The teachers and students here were so *involved* in what they were doing.

Just walking around, Joe and Ralph could not see the lightning, but they could sense that it was there.

Teachers and students moved with purpose. They worked with purpose. They talked with purpose. There was a quiet hustle and bustle throughout the place.

"This is Frank Zendo," Cindy said, pointing out a young man holding a computer diskette. Ralph and Joe noticed right away that this was the same man who, in the 12th Dimension, had worn the armor. Frank told them a little bit about what he taught. Then Cindy said, "Frank found a *dragon* of a problem in our computer laboratory. He kept trying one thing after another to fix it. He thought it had him beat this afternoon, but we talked for a while, and he went back and kept trying until he found the solution. We're all very proud of him."

Just then, the woman who had ridden off on the silver horse came through the door.

"Here comes Susan," said Cindy. "Some of our students are preparing an art project and needed some special materials. Even though Susan isn't a teacher— she's our secretary—she took it upon herself to help out so that the project could be finished on time. Susan found out where the materials could be purchased and then drove into town to pick them up."

They could almost hear *The Lone Ranger* theme playing again.

Then they went to a classroom where some students were talking and working together.

Not wanting to interrupt them, Cindy spoke softly: "This is a student team we put together to come up with ways to increase student participation in school activities. We think it will be a real *diamond mine* for us in terms of student learning and enjoyment."

Finally, Cindy showed them a room where teachers and parents were working together to put on a student production of *Macbeth*. Some had theatrical experience—most did not—but all were contributing as they hammered out a workable plan that would involve the greatest possible number of students. Parents were highly involved, creating sets and costumes, helping students learn their lines, applying makeup, and helping to handle the details of the cast party. Everyone seemed excited about the project, knowing that the students were gaining an appreciation of literature and the theater.

"You really have something special going on here in your school," Ralph said to Cindy.

"Well, we have a lean staff, but our test scores indicate we are on the right track, our students and parents are satisfied, and the quality of our teaching is excellent. Things keep getting better, too," Cindy explained. "I'd say we must be doing a few things right. I'm quite proud of our teachers and students. And our parents too. We want to reach the *zenith* of our potential."

Joe noticed that he was beginning to feel more than a slight twinge of envy. What was it that made Cindy's school so good? Did she have some kind of advantage nobody else had?

"You must have your choice of excellent teachers to do as well as you do," suggested Joe.

"No, I just work with the teachers personnel sends me," said Cindy.

"Then you must have better equipment and resources than everybody else," said Joe.

"Look around," laughed Cindy. "We have the same computers and teaching resources every other elementary school has."

"Better textbooks and manuals then?" asked Joe, getting desperate. "Smarter students? More parent involvement?"

"I wish we did," said Cindy. "But we have the same books and manuals as everybody else in the district, and our parents and students are the same as everywhere else."

"Then what *are* you doing that makes this school so good?" asked Joe.

"Well, it's only partly what *I* do. It's what we *all* do," she explained.

"I know what it is!" exclaimed Ralph. "It's the lightning—!"

For this outburst, Ralph got Joe's elbow poked in his ribs.

"The *what?*" asked Cindy incredulously.

"Nothing," said Joe. "He just means that everybody seems so *energized* around here."

"Oh," said Cindy. "Well, I do think everyone feels good about being here. And I do my best to keep them charged up."

"And just how do you do that?" asked Joe, leaning forward.

"I'd like to think it's just being a good principal," she answered.

This reply definitely did not satisfy Principal Joe, but by now Joe, Ralph, Sophie, and Benjamin were at the door. The tour was over. They thanked Cindy for her time, and the four of them headed back to Normal.

8

Normal Middle School was operating normally when the four returned to Joe's office. Teachers were in the outer office, and the conversations were normal for Normal.

"How much time before the dismissal bell rings?" someone was asking. "Another 10 minutes? I'll never make it!"

Someone else was saying, "Who cares? They're in an assembly the rest of the day. Let the other teachers worry about them."

Near the door, a third voice was saying, "Hey, you're a day early with your report. Slow down or you'll make the rest of us look bad."

And over in the corner, "They don't pay us enough to straighten up our rooms. We should complain to Phyllis about the janitors not doing their job. Where is the principal? He's never around. Bet he went home early. Wish I had a job like that. I'd like to see him try to teach these kids. That's where the real work is."

Assistant Principal Phyllis was trying to explain to a teacher that the copy machine couldn't be repaired until tomorrow.

"Well," said the teacher, "that's *your* problem. I need a hundred copies of this by first thing in the morning!" With that, she hurried out of the office, talking to herself.

Just then, all the teachers noticed that the boss was back, and the whole place went silent. One by one, the teachers rushed out of the office.

"I'm glad you're back," said Phyllis with a sigh of relief.

Joe hurried Sophie and Benjamin off to the pep assembly, and Ralph headed for his science lab.

Ralph was feeling good about himself. His invention was finished, and it had worked. He knew he had created something important and special—an entirely new way of looking at education. He had shown it to his principal, and his principal had seemed impressed. So had Sophie and Benjamin. "Things are going to work out fine," Ralph thought to himself.

But it was not to be.

Back in Ralph's lab, Mary Ellen Krabofski was just getting up from the floor. Her yelling began the moment she laid eyes on Ralph.

What was this stupid contraption she had stumbled into? Had the principal approved it? Did the superintendent know about it? If not, why wasn't the Central Office aware of it—after all, they were supposed to know *everything* about *everything*. What kind of a principal was Joe Mode for allowing unauthorized projects at

Normal? Didn't Ralph Rosco know that extension cords were not allowed by the fire marshall's office? Things certainly had not been like this when she had taught.

"Send for the principal!" shouted Mary Ellen.

Gladly, Ralph did this, so that someone else would have to deal with her.

Principal Joe arrived, and Mary Ellen went on and on. She even mentioned that Workers' Comp might be paying for her hurt foot. In the end, Ralph got the worst of it. He was forbidden to work on his crazy device ever again. In fact, he was ordered to dismantle it before the end of the next day of classes. He was to receive a letter of reprimand from the Central Office, and Joe was to watch his every step.

Ralph reluctantly did as he was told and started to dismantle the Ralpholator.

Joe headed for his office, passing Mrs. Estello, who was on the phone saying, "Magazine order? How should I know? Oh, all right. I'll transfer you to someone else . . . oops!"

Joe looked at Mrs. Estello, and Mrs. Estello looked at Joe. It had been a long day for both of them.

"I guess we were disconnected," said Mrs. Estello. "Oh, well."

"*Nope, no lightning here,*" thought Joe.

He went into his office and sat down at his desk. As soon as he looked at it, Joe felt as if the printout from Mary Ellen had exploded in his face. But the day had not been a total waste. Because Joe had seen lightning. Human lightning. He had seen the Zapp!

9

The end of the day was Joe's thinking time. The students and faculty had left for the day, and the building was quiet.

Why, he wondered, if he was running Normal Middle School in a normal way, did his teachers and students care only about dismissal time? At Zenith Elementary School, Cindy Marks' teachers and students really cared about learning.

Why did he keep getting yelled at by Mary Ellen for not being good enough, while Cindy was delivering great performance?

What was Cindy Marks doing that he was not?

Well, whatever it was, Cindy had the kind of school environment Joe wanted at Normal.

Surely it had to do with the lightning bouncing back and forth among teachers and students. What was that lightning? What made it work?

Then Joe realized, "Hmmmm, this could be it . . . the answer to my problems."

Joe got out his notebook.

JOE MODE'S NOTEBOOK

If I figure out what the lightning is,
then:

- I can use it in my school.
- Students will learn more and be
  happier.
- Teaching will be more fun.
- Maybe Mary Ellen will lighten up.
- Life will be simpler—and better.
- I could become an outstanding
  educator.
- I might even get a promotion!

"And if *she* can do it, *I* can do it!" thought Joe.
But how?

Of course, the easy thing to do would have been to
go to Cindy, talk with her directly and openly, and try
to learn from her.

"Nah!" Joe entertained that possibility for only a

split second. That would have violated his Three Iron-clad Rules:

1. Never ask for help.
2. Never let it seem that you can't handle everything on your own.
3. And never, ever talk to anyone about anything important unless you have no choice.

Besides, if he could do this on his own, he might be able to grab all the credit for it. So Joe decided he would figure it out by himself. The first thing he did was to give the lightning a name.

He called it Zapp!

JOE MODE'S NOTEBOOK

Zapp! . . .

A force that energizes people.

Now, how could he generate Zapp! at Normal Middle School? The problem was that you couldn't see

Zapp!, but it was there. Kind of like excitement and enthusiasm. Joe remembered that at Zenith Elementary School, the teachers and students had seemed proud of what they were doing.

"Aha!" thought Joe. "Cindy must give them pep talks. She must be a motivator."

So the next day, Joe called a brief faculty meeting and tried giving a pep talk. He told the teachers to give their students pep talks, too.

But nothing much happened. A few teachers seemed enthusiastic for about five minutes; then everyone went back to being the way they had been before.

Joe did some more thinking. "Hmmmm. Cindy was nice to everybody," he thought. "So I'll try to be a nice guy for a while."

But that didn't work either. Most people were nice in return, but nobody did a better job or became more committed to their work as a result.

"Well, no more Mr. Nice Guy," thought Joe. "If being nice didn't make any lightning, then I'll be Mr. Mean!"

But being Mr. Mean turned out to be no more effective than being Mr. Nice Guy. Actually, it made things worse. Both the professional staff and the service personnel jumped when Joe appeared, only to slack off when he turned his back. Tensions ran high. Attitudes plummeted. Grievances soared.

Not only that, but after Joe did some checking around, he learned that it was extremely rare for Cindy Marks to raise her voice to any of her teachers or staff members. Yet her teachers and staff applied themselves, got things done on time with outstanding results, and accepted responsibility.

What could he do next?

Then, Joe thought, "Hey, I bet Zapp! is nothing more than one of those new programs the district is always promoting!"

He looked into it and, indeed, Zenith Elementary School did have innovative programs involving teachers, parents, and students. But then, Normal Middle School—and other schools—had them too.

So, it seemed to Joe, special programs were not the same as Zapp!

By now, Joe was stymied. So he decided to visit the resource room in the Central Office. He came across an educational journal on one of the dusty shelves. It mentioned something called "participative management."

It said:

What Ever Happened to Participative Management?

Participative management stems from the idea of involving all personnel in the decision-making process. Sometimes it is called "employee involvement." The basic idea has been around for a long time, but it's had its ups and downs in terms of popularity.

One of the big problems is that hardly anybody understands what it really means. In the Fifties, principals thought it meant being friendly to teachers and staff. In the Sixties, they thought it meant being sensitive to the needs and motivations of people. In the Seventies, school administrators thought it meant asking teachers and parents for help. In the Eighties and Nineties, it meant having lots of group meetings involving everybody.

Using it, different administrators get different results. One administrator calls a meeting and tries to get people involved—and it works. Another administrator does the same thing—and nothing happens.

While participative management has not been a failure, confusion over what it is (and what it is not) has prevented widespread success.

Could Zenith Elementary School be using participative management? Joe wasn't sure. Normal Middle School had student, teacher, and parent advisory groups. Wasn't that participative management? He was confused.

Then Joe read something about job satisfaction and job enrichment programs and various other kinds of programs. But he was sure Zenith Elementary School had none of these, or he would have heard about them at the regular principals' meetings.

Maybe it had something to do with the way Normal School District was organized.

The entire district had gone through a reorganization last year that had involved the removal of some of the Central Office administrators. In the district's newsletter, the superintendent had called it a "flattened" staff organization. According to the superintendent, reorganization was supposed to be a good thing. But everyone in the schools knew that the real reason it had happened was because of reduced funding.

All Joe knew was that soon after the flattening process began, *he* nearly had been flattened by the weight of new responsibilities dropped on him, and he had almost lost his assistant principal. It appeared to Joe that if there were good things about a flattened organization, only Zenith Elementary School seemed to know about them.

Then Joe considered things like staff development, good communication, closer teacher-administrator relationships, special-interest classes for students, and lots of other ideas.

In every case, if Zenith Elementary School had them, they worked. If the other schools had them, they didn't seem to matter much.

Now Joe was really stumped. Nearly all the ideas he'd considered were, he had to admit, very good ones. So he made a list.

JOE MODE'S NOTEBOOK

Schools have tried:

- Better communication.
- Closer principal-teacher relationships.
- Local school-improvement teams.
- Parent-teacher committees.
- Sabbatical leaves.
- Employment of consultants.
- Community resource people.
- School partnerships with businesses.
- Computer-assisted instruction.
- Improved quality-of-work-life programs.
- Curriculum councils.
- School visitation programs.
- Effective school programs.
- Staff-development programs.

NOTEBOOK ▦ (cont'd)

• Faculty senates.
• And lots of other programs.

What happened?

• Results were usually mixed,
  short-lived, disappointing, counter-
  productive, confusing, or
  insignificant—in most of the school
  district.
• They work well only when Zenith
  Elementary School tries them.

Now what did that mean?

"That Zenith Elementary School has the *key* to making all these other ideas and programs work, something we're still missing!" Joe concluded.

"That must be the lightning," thought Joe. "Whatever that Zapp! is, it's got to be powerful stuff."

He got out his notebook.

JOE MODE'S NOTEBOOK

Zapp! . . .

A key to success for new ideas and programs.

They work with Zapp!

They fail without Zapp!

But at this point, Joe saw that he was still no closer to understanding what Zapp! was. He knew that he needed help. So he decided to violate Ironclad Rule Number One.

10

By now, Ralph Rosco was back in his normal routine. And because of the letter of reprimand, he really hated to go to school every day.

The Teachers' Association, of course, had filed a grievance on his behalf, but that was an endless bureaucratic voyage, and Ralph wasn't sure he wanted to go that route. Right now, he just wanted to be left alone by everyone, especially school administrators.

Meanwhile, his attitude was abysmally negative, and he walked around like a zombie until quitting time. This was not a good time to talk to Ralph about much of anything that had to do with school.

But Joe Mode knew that he needed help, and that Ralph was the only one in the school who would understand what he was talking about.

So he went to Ralph one day near dismissal time.

"Look, Ralph, I want to figure out what that lightning was in Cindy Marks' school. I can't do it on my own, and I was wondering if you'd help me."

"You want *me* to help *you*? Forget it!" shouted Ralph.

"OK," said Joe. "I admit you got a bad break. But if you'll help me out on this, I'll submit your invention to the Central Office for approval."

"Take it to the Central Office? Ha!" said Ralph. "Don't make me laugh! They won't do anything except bury it in some committee."

"But think about it," encouraged Joe. "To help me, you'll have to reassemble your Ralpholator. You can start using it again, and it'll be with my blessing. That way, I'll take the blame if Mary Ellen Krabofski is unhappy."

"Well . . ." said Ralph.

"And if we can figure out what the lightning is and what makes it go Zapp!, then we can use it here in our school, and you'll have been a part of that."

"Well . . ." said Ralph.

"And later on, I'll even try to get you a free period so you can keep developing your machine. You said you thought this was important, that it could help us help students. What do you say? Are we going to work together on this?"

"Well . . ." said Ralph. "OK!"

Then they shook hands, both genuinely excited. At that moment, had they been able to observe what was going on from the 12th Dimension, they would have seen a very small bolt of lightning flash between them.

11

Ralph hurried to school the next morning with new interest and vitality. He even whistled as he left his car, heading toward the Normal entrance. He was happy for a change. "Maybe I can make a difference," he thought.

Once inside the building, he even decided not to stop in the faculty lounge because he had a task to complete: the Ralpholator.

Ralph held a very short meeting with his student teacher, approved her lesson plans for the week, and checked with her to see how things were going. He was pleased to hear that Philip and Sarah were keeping up with the rest of the students. Following Ralph's example, Mandy had been devoting one of her free periods to helping Philip and Sarah. Just as Ralph had discovered, she found that the extra attention was helping these two students keep up with the rest of their class.

Ralph was pleased with Mandy's teaching ability, but there was something else that had impressed him even more: She truly *cared* about her students.

Mandy was doing quite well, and Ralph was glad. Not only because Mandy was helping the students learn, but because her competence gave him some free time to work on his special project.

Once in his lab, Ralph quickly reassembled the Ralpholator, fired it up, and vanished into the 12th Dimension.

As he wandered around the school, the Normal situation was still normal. Everyone was the same . . . dim and gloomy, with all the charm of a minimum security prison.

In the midst of all this was Joe Mode, dressed that day (to the eyes of those in the 12th Dimension) in a cowboy hat, boots, and spurs. He was toting a six-gun, ready to blast anyone who got in his way.

Ralph was about to walk over to Zenith Elementary School when he saw something he had not noticed before.

Ralph watched as Joe walked up to Donna, the teacher who was wrapped in mummy tape. Soon after Joe started talking, there was a flash of—well, it was not lightning.

Instead of a flash of light, there was a flash of night.

Kind of like blinking your eyes.

And there was a sound.

It did not go Zapp!

It went "Ssssapp¡"

To Ralph, it sounded like a balloon deflating. After the Sapp¡ happened, Ralph watched as a couple of more turns of mummy tape wound around Donna, making the light inside her a shade dimmer.

Then Ralph noticed the custodian trying to say something to Joe. Joe walked away, not paying any attention to her.

Sapp¡

The custodian became even more zombie-like.

About that time, Sophie entered the office. She had just won an award and wanted to tell her principal the good news, but he didn't have time to listen. He said only "Good girl" as he turned and walked away from her. Sophie left the office with her head lowered.

Sapp¡

Next, Ralph heard Joe tell Phyllis how to do a job she had done many times before, without bothering to listen to how *she* thought it should be done.

Sapp¡

And a fresh new sandbag appeared on the growing fortifications around her desk.

Ralph then saw Joe rush over to someone who was having a problem, immediately pull him off the job, and start solving the problem himself.

Sapp¡

But it wasn't just what Joe was doing. It was also what he was *not* doing. Ralph heard some of the teachers complaining that they had no idea how well they were teaching.

"Principal Mode was supposed to evaluate all of us last month," explained Sam. "But then he didn't—he said he had other, more important things to do."

Sapp¡

The teachers were even doing it to each other. He

heard one teacher telling some others, "That's not our problem. Let the principal worry about it."

Sapp¡

Worst of all were the comments teachers were making to the students.

"Gary, I don't have time to listen to your excuses. You know the rules—either straighten up, or I'll have to send you to the principal's office."

Sapp¡

And "There you go again, whining like a baby. Please, Bobbi, can't you be more like your older sister?"

Sapp¡

"What's going on here?" Ralph wondered. These were routine, everyday, *normal* occurrences—nothing that most people would notice.

But whenever these things happened, people got dimmer and slower instead of brighter and faster.

Sometimes, a few new stones would appear on the maze of walls crisscrossing the hallway, or a new chain would wrap itself around someone's arm or leg, or some other restraint would form.

Whatever was happening, it was keeping teachers and students divided and confined, draining their energy or damming it up so it couldn't be used.

And Joe Mode was a big part of it. He went through the day Sapping people left and right. And in the same way he Sapped his teachers, the teachers Sapped their students.

"He's like a black hole, absorbing energy from

everyone who works for him," thought Ralph.

By the end of the day, throughout most of Normal, the majority of teachers and students were dull and de-energized. When the light from the opening door streaked in at quitting time, everybody bolted for it, glad that the day was over.

Ralph watched them go, rushing for the fix of energy they needed from home and family and the things they did *after* school. He wandered back through the fog toward Joe's office. When he got there, he saw that Joe was in trouble.

Joe was alone in the midst of an enormous cloud of flashing night. He was beaten and bruised, cowboy hat lost, standing his ground as jaws and claws came out of the fog from all directions. He had been bravely firing away with his six-guns at a many-faced thing. Though his bullets had wounded some of the monsters, there were many more than he could shoot at, and his guns were now empty.

What was this thing confronting Joe? Ralph stood and watched him fight his losing battle. And then Ralph had a hunch what it was.

It was everything Joe had Sapped from everyone else. What Joe had taken away, had not shared, was now beating him. What was it?

It was Responsibility.

It was Authority.

It was Identity.

It was Challenge.

It was Trust.

12

Of course, Joe Mode did not believe any of this stuff about Sapp¡ and the cowboy hat and six-guns.

"Then go take a look for yourself," Ralph challenged. "It's not just in your school. It's in the whole school system."

Joe walked to Ralph's lab. After entering the proper commands on the Ralpholator, he entered the 12th Dimension. Invisible to the normal world, Joe walked through Normal Middle School.

He saw a teacher who was supposed to be leading a class discussion. But there was no discussion. The teacher was doing all the talking. Even when the teacher asked a question, he jumped in and told the students the answer. The teacher seemed to enjoy hearing himself talk, but the students were bored.

Sapp¡

In another classroom, he overheard a student asking Mrs. Poorly, a French teacher, how she'd done on last week's test. Immediately, several other students were asking the same question. They'd all studied hard for the test and were anxious to know how they'd done.

"Oh, I don't know," answered Mrs. Poorly. "I already had a grade for you last week. I've had a lot of other papers to grade this week. Maybe we'll just forget that test."

Sapp¡

In a mathematics department meeting, he saw Mr. Milton, the chairperson, taking all the credit for a good idea—an idea that one of the other math teachers had come up with.

Sapp¡

Walking into the faculty lounge, Joe stopped at a bulletin board where two teachers were reading his latest memo. "Henceforth," the memo read, "all teachers are to report to the principal's office upon arrival each morning. Your arrival time will be recorded and monitored." As teachers read Joe's memo, they walked away, silently.

Sapp¡

Joe went into the guidance office and found a counselor talking with an angry parent. Tiny beads of sweat were breaking out on the counselor's forehead because the parent's complaint was administrative in nature, not related to counseling. The parent had been told by Joe to meet with the counselor because the principal didn't want to take time to handle the problem. The counselor, who realized she had no authority to make an administrative decision, just had to sit there and take it.

Sapp¡

Coming up the stairwell were two teachers who were upset because of the new activities schedule Joe had posted yesterday. One of them said, "I had an important field trip that will have to be cancelled because of the new schedule. Mr. Mode didn't even check with me to see if the new schedule would work."

The other teacher nodded her head. "That's normal for Normal," she said.

Sappį Sappįį

Joe Mode went into the gym. He saw the activities coordinator, the basketball coach, and the wrestling coach standing by a desk discussing their team schedules and practice times.

"Every time the gym is used for some special event, it's a big hassle to get it set up again," the wrestling coach complained. "The maintenance workers always seem to forget about moving our mats. They held up a match the other evening by half an hour because they were late. What can be done about this?"

"Well," sighed the activities coordinator, "there's not much I can do about these problems if the principal won't listen. But I'll try one more time to arrange a meeting with him."

"These problems occur every couple of weeks," complained the upset coach. "It seems nobody in this school cares about our activities."

"Do the best you can for a while until we can have the meeting. But remember, Principal Mode probably will not have time for us."

As the activities coordinator walked away, the basketball coach said, "That's normal. He never has time to listen."

"What's the use?" the wrestling coach agreed.

Sapp¡

Joe continued his tour. Overall, he saw lots of Sapping and not very much Zapping going on.

When Joe came back to the normal world, he sat down with Ralph and told him what he'd seen in the 12th Dimension. Together, they came up with quite a list of what Sapps people.

JOE MODE'S NOTEBOOK

Examples of what Sapps people:

- Lack of responsibility.
- Meaningless work.
- Someone else solving problems for you.
- Assignments that are always the same.
- No way of determining how well others think you're doing.
- No way of measuring your own performance.
- No challenge.
- No authority.
- No time to solve problems.
- Lack of trust.
- Not being listened to.
- Not getting credit for your ideas or efforts.

NOTEBOOK 📓 (cont'd)

- Believing that you can't make a difference.
- Rigid, bureaucratic policies.
- Confusion.
- Not enough knowledge or skills to do the job.
- Lack of support, coaching, and feedback.
- Poor communication.
- Not enough resources to do the job well.
- People treated exactly the same, like interchangeable parts.

"Look," Joe said, after scanning the list. "Don't a lot of these examples have something in common?"

"Most of them have to do with confidence and trust—or, rather, the lack of them," said Ralph.

"And self-esteem and control," said Joe.

"If the lack of these things Sapps people," said Ralph, "I wonder what more confidence and trust, higher esteem, and less control would do?"

They looked at each other. Had they found the secret?

It was about then that Joe and Ralph began to realize that Sapp¡ and Zapp! were halves of the same idea.

JOE MODE'S NOTEBOOK

Zapp!—the giving of power?
Sapp¡—the taking of power?

13

The next morning, at the start of the third period, Sophie and Benjamin went to see Ralph Rosco in the lab. The Ralpholator was hooked up, which made Sophie hesitant to enter the room. Benjamin, of course, went straight for the machine.

Ralph soon learned from the two students that the school counselor had told Sophie and Benjamin they needed to choose their science classes for high school. Both students liked science, but they had heard many stories about the difficulty of science classes at the high school and were a bit apprehensive.

After telling Ralph their dilemma, they said they wanted to know how hard the different high school science classes were before discussing the options with their parents. They really needed his help.

Then Benjamin, bright eyed and bushy tailed, pleaded with Ralph to visit the high school by way of the Ralpholator. Even Sophie liked the idea. Benjamin begged, "Please, Mr. Rosco, take us. If Mr. Mode were here, he would go along."

Ralph liked the idea, especially since he had just invented a new control for the Ralpholator. It was a module that controlled the direction and distance of travel in the 12th Dimension. What was really exciting was that he could use the new remote control to move from one place to another in the 12th Dimension without returning to the lab.

Just then Joe Mode came through the door. Hearing Sophie and Benjamin's request, he became excited too, because he had been wondering what was going on at Typical High School. He figured that while Sophie and Benjamin checked out the science classes, he and Ralph could look around the rest of the school.

Ralph agreed and, after a few adjustments, they all took their turns entering the 12th Dimension. Right on target, they found themselves in the main corridor of the high school.

Sophie and Benjamin headed off to the science department to check things out, and Ralph and Joe decided to walk around.

The first classroom Joe and Ralph walked into was an English literature class where the students were discussing some short stories by O'Henry. Joe and Ralph were surprised to see that the teacher was seated at the rear of the classroom, and *a student* was leading the discussion.

"What's this?" whispered Joe.

"Let's stay and find out," answered Ralph.

To Joe and Ralph's amazement, the student leading the discussion asked questions about *The Gift of the*

Magi—and the students gave lots of interesting, well-thought-out answers.

What was the main point of the story?

How were the characters developed?

Why was the ending surprising?

If the students got stuck, or began getting off track, the teacher would help get the class going in the right direction. But the teacher didn't give the answers herself.

Instead, she helped *the class* discover the answers.

Zapp!

"Hmmm," said Joe out loud. "I wonder if that would work at Normal. . . ."

"Let's go look in on some other classes," suggested Ralph.

They walked down the hall until they came to the home ec room. There they saw boys and girls sitting in groups of four or five, discussing their upcoming projects.

One group was deciding what types of foods they'd like to prepare over the next few weeks. Another group was discussing how they would distribute cookies they made to a nearby retirement home over the holidays. And a third group was talking about the nutritional needs of high school students.

As the different groups talked, the teacher moved from group to group, listening or making suggestions, depending on the group's needs.

"Great idea, Mike," said the teacher, smiling. "You're on the right track."

Zapp!

As the teacher moved from group to group, little bolts of lightning flickered among the students.

"Wow!" exclaimed Ralph excitedly. "I think we're on to something!"

Joe and Ralph went back out into the hallway and decided to keep exploring. They liked what they'd seen, and they wanted to see more.

As they turned left down the corridor, they saw a teacher scolding a group of students.

"*Because I said so!*" yelled the teacher. "Rules are rules—that's why!"

The students looked frustrated and confused. But the teacher just continued, "Now go back to your seats—and this time do what I tell you to do!"

Sapp¡

Joe and Ralph turned to look at one another. "What's going on?" Ralph asked Joe. "Could different things be going on in the same school?"

"It sure looks that way," answered Joe. "Let's go find Sophie and Benjamin."

"Follow me," called Ralph. "The science department is this way."

As they rounded the bend, Joe and Ralph saw students coming out of the planetarium, beaming with excitement. Others, coming from a zoology class, looked bored and gloomy. Some of the teachers were radiating light, while others were dim and colorless.

Sophie and Benjamin walked over to their principal and science teacher.

"We've checked out four different classes," explained Sophie. "And some look a lot more fun than others."

"Yeah," agreed Benjamin. "One of the teachers seems so mean! But most of them are pretty nice."

Then Joe suggested they walk down to the principal's office. "I'd like to see how she operates Typical High School," he said.

Principal Smith, though, was busy worrying about her many problems. The band parents wanted to have a bingo night to raise money for the band's annual trip to Walt Disney World. The Football Booster Club members were upset with the coach for benching a star player because of his low grades. The vocational teachers were complaining about having to come in on Sunday to prepare their labs for open house. And several angry parents were waiting to talk with the principal.

"There are some hot spots here, but the school doesn't glow like Zenith Elementary," Joe said. "Let's go back to Normal."

With the help of Ralph's new remote control, they were soon back at Normal Middle School. Sophie and Benjamin left for their next classes, and Joe and Ralph talked. What was it that made some teachers effective and others not? What was it that Cindy Marks was doing at Zenith that they weren't doing at Normal and Typical?

It was time for Ralph to take another look at Zenith Elementary School.

14

Ralph spent the next day invisibly observing Zenith Elementary School from the 12th Dimension. He wanted to learn more about how people feel when they are Zapped and Sapped.

Immediately he saw that there was plenty of Zapp! going around. But it was hard to see why it was happening. Still, he observed some big differences between Cindy Marks' school and Normal Middle School.

In Zenith Elementary School, the teachers pretty much ran their own classrooms. They could make a lot of decisions on their own.

At Normal, everybody had to check with Joe before doing anything.

The teachers at Zenith acted as if their jobs were important to them and they were important to their jobs.

Teachers at Normal Middle School acted as if their jobs didn't much matter in the scheme of things.

Whether things went right or wrong, the teachers took it a bit personally at Zenith.

It was hard to know if things were right or wrong at Normal. No matter how things went, the teachers there thought it was bad to take things personally or to get personally involved.

The teachers at Zenith were so involved with their teaching that they talked about it with one another—sometimes even during the lunch period.

The teachers at Normal would look at you oddly if you said anything about your teaching that indicated personal involvement. The only acceptable topics during casual conversations were family matters, vacations, sports, and hobbies.

At Cindy Marks' school, the day ended when you finished that day's tasks. Then each teacher left with a sense of accomplishment—tired, but still energized—and *wanting* to come back tomorrow.

At Normal Middle School, the day ended when the dismissal bell sounded, and the teachers hurried out, counting the days left to the weekend, retirement, or both.

After a while in the 12th Dimension, Ralph began to get an idea of how teachers and staff members felt when they were Sapped and when they were Zapped. When he got back to Normal, he talked to Principal Mode, and they entered their new insights into Joe's notebook.

JOE MODE'S NOTEBOOK

When you have been Sapped, you feel like:

- Your job belongs to the district.
- You are just taking orders.
- You always have to keep your mouth shut.
- Your job doesn't really matter.
- You don't know how well you're doing.
- You have little or no control over your work.
- Your job is different from who you are.

JOE MODE'S NOTEBOOK

When you have been Zapped, you feel like:

• Your job belongs to you.

• You are responsible.

• You have some say in how things are done.

• Your job counts for something.

• You know where you stand.

• You have some control over your work.

• Your job is a part of who you are.

After much discussion, Joe and Ralph came up with some examples of what Zapps people. As they talked, Joe scribbled in his notebook.

"We figured out what Sapps people. Now I think we know what Zapps people," said Joe.

JOE MODE'S NOTEBOOK

Examples of what Zapps people:

- Responsibility.
- Meaningful work.
- Solving problems as a team.
- Variety in assignments.
- Measurable outputs.
- Ability to measure your own performance.
- Challenge.
- Authority to commit yourself.
- Having the time to solve problems.
- Trust.
- Being listened to.
- Praise.
- Recognition for ideas.
- Knowing why you're important to the system.

NOTEBOOK (cont'd)

- Flexible controls.
- Direction (knowing what's important and how much or what quality is wanted).
- Knowledge and skills to do the job (training, staff development, continuing education, and relevant information).
- Support, coaching, and feedback.
- Effective communication in all directions.
- Resources readily available.
- People treated like individuals, not like interchangeable parts.

They were definitely discovering something important.

Joe and Ralph were pleased with their discoveries. But they wondered what they could *do* with them.

PART II

The Zapping of Normal
Middle School

15

Joe was excited about what he and Ralph had found out. He was thinking about how he could create more Zapp! at Normal, when his phone began to ring.

"Hi, it's me," said Ralph, when Joe answered.

"I was just about to come see you," said Joe.

"But I'm not in my office. I'm standing next to you in your office in the 12th Dimension, only you can't see me."

"Then how are you talking to me?"

"With my new cellular Ralphophone—the only telephone that works in the 12th Dimension," said Ralph. "I invented the new backpack model so that I wouldn't have to keep going back to the normal world to talk to you."

"That's great," said Joe who, as usual, had no time for chitchat. "I have figured it out. It's simple. Zapped people own their jobs, they're responsible, they make decisions on their own—right? So I'll have everybody here be like that."

"But how?" asked Ralph.

"Easy," said Joe. "I'll just call a meeting and tell them that's the way it's going to be."

Pushing all doubts aside, Joe immediately went to the school's PA system and announced that there would be a special, very short meeting for all faculty and staff at the end of the day. Joe was quite proud of himself and spent the next hour thinking about how easy it would be to make Normal more like Zenith.

Soon after the dismissal bell, Joe hurried to the auditorium to face a tired and provoked faculty and staff, who were upset because of the timing of the meeting.

Joe quickly called the meeting to order. Then, with a smile, he stated, "I have great news for all of you. Things are going to change at Normal. So listen up, everybody. From now on, you own your jobs. They're all yours. I'm not making any decisions for you. You're responsible for everything that has to do with your teaching or your other responsibilities. Each of you can decide how you want to get your work done. You're in control. From this moment forward, I have complete confidence in all of you. Oh, by the way, your jobs are important, so start acting like it. And make sure the students are happy. Any questions?"

Of course, there were no questions because nobody understood what in the world he was talking about.

"Good. Everyone have a nice evening," said Joe.

Having made his speech, Joe returned to his office, put his feet up on his desk, and daydreamed fantasies of

Central Office's congratulations—and maybe even awards—for his great idea.

A few minutes later, Ralph called and said, "Joe, I hate to tell you this, but I don't think things will go very well tomorrow. You confused and upset everyone at the meeting."

"What? Wasn't everybody Zapped after my speech?" asked Joe.

"You'd better take a look for yourself tomorrow morning."

And indeed, Ralph was right. As soon as school started the next morning, Normal was not normal. In fact, it was in a state of chaos.

One teacher decided that a half-day field trip to a museum would be educational for her students, and off she went without coordinating the revised schedule with the students' other teachers. The cooks decided to change the menu that the school dietician had developed, but they didn't have all the ingredients they needed. Several coaches decided to lengthen the after-school practice period without considering how the students would get home. And one bus driver decided to change his schedule—effective that very morning.

All around the school, arguments were breaking out among the teachers and the service personnel. They all wanted to do things *their* way.

But most people were carrying on exactly as before, as if Joe's proclamation had never been made. After spending all their teaching and working lives in a state of Sapp¡, nobody knew what to do.

Joe hurriedly got the teachers and students into their classrooms and told everyone just to be normal, although he wasn't quite sure what that meant. He sent Assistant Principal Phyllis to deal with the cafeteria and bus problems, and he returned to his office with another headache. Then he decided to call a short faculty and staff meeting during the lunch period—something that was not normal at Normal.

Somehow the morning ended without any riots or casualties. As the noon bell sounded, Joe hurried to the staff meeting and announced, "Remember what I said yesterday? Well, forget it. From now on, I'm back in charge. You're dismissed."

Now everyone was doubly Sapped.

The whole matter was trickier than Joe Mode had figured. He retreated to his office and made an entry in his notebook.

JOE MODE'S NOTEBOOK

It is easy to Sapp¡
It is hard to Zapp!

"Now what do I do?!" he asked aloud as he paced back and forth. "If I can't *talk* people into being Zapped, how can I make it happen?"

A moment later the phone rang. It was Ralph, who had just entered the 12th Dimension. He was in Joe's office and could hear everything Joe was saying.

"You know, Joe, I've never seen Cindy try to *talk* people into being Zapped. I don't think that's how she does it."

"Then what does she do?" asked Joe.

"Well . . ." said Ralph, "I'm not sure exactly."

"OK, we're going to figure this out one way or another," said Joe. "You go to Zenith Elementary School, find Cindy, and follow her around. Find out *exactly* what she does."

So Ralph did just that.

An hour later, Joe's phone rang again. It was Ralph with his first observation to report.

Ralph had been watching Cindy and noticed that whenever she talked to someone, she didn't put the person down or make the person feel inferior. Even if there was a problem, she said what she had to say so that people still felt, if not great, at least OK about themselves. That is, she always *maintained or enhanced the person's self-esteem*.

"OK, I'll try that out," said Joe. "You follow me now and watch what happens."

Joe thought for a moment and then went out into the hallway. The first person he came to was Helen, a social studies teacher.

"Helen, you're a very snappy dresser," said Joe. "I especially like how your shoes always match and how your dresses and scarves never clash."

Then Joe saw Don, a math teacher, and said, "Don, you play a fantastic game of softball. I saw you play in the faculty game the other evening."

To this, Don said, "Gee, thanks, Joe."

"But you know, Don, you screwed up royally in how you handled that parent complaint last week. I had to spend two hours getting the woman settled down. I suggest you shape up and never let it happen again."

Then Joe went back to his office and waited for Ralph to call and tell him how he did.

"When you talked to Helen, nothing happened. No lightning, no Zapp!, nothing," said Ralph. "And when you talked to Don, you actually Sapped him."

"Why? I said nice things to both of them. Didn't that do anything for their self-esteem?"

"But Joe, you didn't say anything positive about their *teaching*. Cindy doesn't go out of her way just to tell people they look nice or that she likes the way they play softball. She talks about things they're doing on the job. And remember, she never puts people down, even if there is a problem."

"OK," said Joe. "Let me try again."

He went back out again, found Helen, and said, "Helen, I like how you keep your classroom clean. You're very well organized, and I'm sure that helps you do quality teaching. Keep it up."

Then he found Don and said, "Don, what I was

really trying to say earlier was that I think you're usually a first-rate teacher. What happened yesterday was a mistake, but I hope you'll keep delivering the kind of teaching you generally do."

At this, Don nodded and said, "I'll try not to let it happen again."

"OK," said Joe. "You're a good teacher, and that's all I can ask."

After each of these conversations, Ralph saw little flickers of lightning. They were small, barely visible, but they were there. He called Joe.

"Bingo!" said Ralph. "You did it! You Zapped 'em!"

A few days passed, and Joe kept using words that would maintain or enhance teachers' self-esteem when he talked to them about their work.

In fact, he tried to say something constructive to each person in the school every day. After all those years of being Sapped, he reasoned, it was going to take a lot of little Zapps to build up a positive charge in the school.

Joe was very careful in what he said, for he was determined to Zapp! as many teachers and staff members as possible. He figured that when his teachers felt capable, responsible, and valued, then they would encourage these same qualities in their students.

Ralph was especially glad to see that the Zapps were filtering down to the students. On one occasion, after Joe had complimented Nan, a language arts teacher, about how well she had organized a field trip for her students, she turned to two of her students, smiled, and then complimented them on their help with the activity. "Was Zapp! contagious?" wondered Ralph.

Ralph also discovered that the quality of what Joe said was important too. People could tell when something he said was insincere or undeserved. In those cases, the Zapp! quickly turned into a Sapp¡

As time went by, Ralph saw the little flickers of lightning at Normal grow brighter. Still, they were small, nothing like the brilliance or size of the Zapps! at Zenith Elementary School.

As Joe returned to his office, he ran into Ralph. "You did a good job observing what Cindy was doing," Joe said to Ralph. "I know we're on the right track. But enhancing self-esteem must be only the first step. Why don't you keep looking and see what else she does?"

Still, Joe felt good about what he had accomplished so far. As the school day ended, he thought for a minute and then pulled his notebook from his desk drawer.

JOE MODE'S NOTEBOOK

1st principle of Zapp!

MAINTAIN OR ENHANCE
SELF-ESTEEM

16

The next morning, after meeting with his student teacher, Ralph pushed the Ralpholator button again and headed for Zenith Elementary School. As he expected, amazing things were going on as usual. Monsters were being tamed, strange and wonderful structures and machines were being created, and new horizons were being entered. And the incredible lightning energizing all of this was Zapping brilliantly from Cindy to her teachers and from the teachers to their students.

Then Ralph noticed something he thought was rather odd. While some of the lightning flashed when Cindy talked, often she would just be there with someone, seemingly doing nothing, and Zapp!—a little bolt of lightning would jump from her to the next person. It was as if Cindy could generate a Zapp! just by standing next to someone.

By now, Ralph knew that Zapp! did not happen by itself. Cindy had to be doing *something*. So he watched her some more.

Then he noticed that Cindy was letting her teachers do the talking. She would stand or sit nearby, often a hand on her chin, eyes focused on the other person, sometimes her head angled to one side. And as she did this, a little Zapp! would pass between her and the person talking.

"What was she doing," Ralph wondered.

Why, of course! She was *listening!*

He got on the Ralphophone, dialed Joe Mode, and told him, "Listening to people is another way to Zapp! them."

"So what's the big deal about that?" asked Joe. "I listen to people all the time."

Ralph did not say anything.

"Don't I listen to people?" asked Joe.

Still Ralph said nothing.

"WELL, DON'T I?"

"Lots of times I'm not sure, Joe," said Ralph.

"And why not?"

"Because you're doing other things while I'm talking, or you don't let me finish what I have to say, or you change the subject when I do finish," said Ralph.

Joe took this in. Then he said, "OK, but how do you know *she's* really listening?"

"Well, because she's looking at the person, and she's nodding her head as if she understands."

"Oh, what the heck, Ralph. My kids do that! And I never know if they're listening or not," said Joe.

"Wait a minute, I know," said Ralph, remembering something that made the lightning glow brighter.

"When the other person was finished talking, she repeated a little summary of what had been said."

"So she really is listening," thought Joe.

"All right, let me try it," he said to Ralph.

And he did.

As soon as he stepped out of his office, Phyllis came over to him and started to talk about a problem she was having with a bus driver.

Joe stood in front of her.

He looked her in the eye.

He focused his full attention on her.

He nodded his head as she made a point.

But after a few seconds, he found that it was hard to listen well. Even though Phyllis got to the point quickly, Joe's own thoughts kept coming faster than her words. His own thoughts seemed to cover up what he was hearing. If he didn't push his own thoughts aside and concentrate on her words, soon he would not hear what she was saying.

When Phyllis was finished, Joe tried to summarize what she had said to let her know he had listened. But he found he had caught only the first part of what she had said.

Still, he tried it some more. That was another thing to Joe Mode's credit: He would always keep trying.

As he went through Normal Middle School, he practiced listening to people the rest of the day. And the next day. And the day after that.

After a while, Joe became pretty good at listening to people. Instead of letting his own thoughts clutter up the message he was hearing, he kept his mind busy with making a mental list of each point the person made. Then it was easy to give back a short summary. If he got a point wrong, the person to whom he had been listening could make the point clear.

Joe noticed something else important: Aside from letting people know he was paying attention to what they said, he also began to understand what was really going on in the school.

Meanwhile, during his free period each day, Ralph used the Ralpholator to see how Joe was doing.

As you might imagine, Ralph was getting a big kick out of checking up on his principal. At first, Ralph, who had his cynical side, figured that Joe Mode would *never* really listen to anybody. He even thought he might have the grim pleasure at the end of the week of telling Joe that the Zapps! were not happening, that Joe would never learn.

But Ralph was wrong.

In fact, to his surprise, Joe was doing quite well. Just by building self-esteem and by listening to people, the Sapps¡ had become far fewer and the Zapps! far more common. There was a weak but definite glow now around the teachers and students at Normal Middle School.

What really came as a surprise was that Ralph did not even have to be in the 12th Dimension to notice it. There was less tension in the school. Problems seemed to get sorted out a little faster. The teachers and students seemed happier.

And yet, he did have to report that the Zapps! Joe gave by listening were not of the magnitude Cindy Marks gave. When Joe listened, the Zapp! would start to grow and glow as hers did. But then Joe would walk away, and the Zapp! would vanish. Sometimes it even became a Sapp¡

One day Ralph was having trouble with a new feature of the Ralpholator. So he told Joe about it.

"I worked all last evening on this, but I just don't have the tools to fix the problem," said Ralph, sounding extremely frustrated.

Joe listened dutifully, nodded his head, and even repeated an accurate summary of what Ralph had said.

Then Joe pivoted and walked away.

"Hey, Joe, wait a minute," Ralph said.

Joe walked back and said, "What?"

"Is that it?" asked Ralph. "Is that all you're going to do?"

"What else do you expect?" asked Joe.

"At least some kind of response," said Ralph.

Joe was puzzled. Hadn't he done the Zapping thing right? Hadn't he listened?

Suddenly Ralph understood why Joe was not generating the maximum charge when he listened.

"Joe, I think there are two parts to this listening thing," said Ralph. "The first part is listening. The second part is responding. You've got the listening part fine, but often you don't respond."

"OK," said Joe. "How about if I say, 'I heard you. Now get back to your classroom.' "

"That makes me feel like you just want to get rid of me," said Ralph. "It's a Sapp¡"

"But I wasn't trying to get rid of you," said Joe. "In fact, I was going to try to get you some help."

"Then why don't you tell me that?" asked Ralph.

To which Joe said, "All right then, how about if I say, 'I heard what you said. I'll get you the help you need.'"

Ralph considered this. "Well, that's a little better, but somehow it feels as though there is still something missing. I mean, I spent my entire evening at school rather than at home trying to work this out, and you didn't even acknowledge that."

Then Joe Mode suddenly got it. He had listened and responded to the words Ralph had said, but not to the *tone* in which Ralph had said them.

"OK, *I sense that you're very frustrated,* and I know that you are giving this project your all—even staying late," said Joe. "Why don't you work on something else, and I'll get you the help you need."

When he said that, there was a Zapp!, one that lasted longer and glowed brighter than before. Joe knew from that point on that he not only had to listen, he had to *respond with empathy*.

From then on, after Joe listened, he tried to give the person an appropriate answer by responding to more than just the actual, factual words. Instead, he also responded to the feelings behind the words.

This meant that Joe had to pay close attention to the context of what was being said, and take into account not only the person's tone of voice, but things like body language, facial expressions, and events leading up to the discussion.

For instance, when someone came to him with a problem, Joe often said something like, "OK, I understand you're upset. Let's try to work something out."

When approached with a request, Joe might say something like, "I sense that this is important to you. We'll see what we can do."

Of course, there were lots of times when nothing could be done. Problems sometimes had to be endured rather than solved; requests sometimes had to be denied.

In those cases, Joe would say something like, "I know this is tough for you, but there's nothing we can do right now. Meanwhile, it's important to the whole school that you hang in there and do the best you can."

Even this registered a Zapp! because Joe's people knew that at least they had been heard and considered. And they knew their principal was with them, not against them.

JOE MODE'S NOTEBOOK

2nd principle of Zapp!

LISTEN AND RESPOND
WITH EMPATHY

17

Some say it came from the Central Office where administrators had tried unsuccessfully to keep it on a leash.

Another thesis is that it had existed for many years—hibernating until awakened by the fanfare accompanying an administrative proclamation of a new educational policy.

And some say it had grown up at Normal—small at first, but growing, slinking about at night, gorging on memos, reports, directives, and other combustibles.

Wherever it came from, it was a big mother dragon. It stalked the Normal halls in the 12th Dimension, looking for places to lay eggs. And the field was fertile.

Ralph saw it one day. He was experimenting with his newest invention, the Zappometer (pronounced "zapp-aw'-met-er"), which measures Sapp¡–Zapp! ratios and lightning levels.

Normal Middle School had become a much brighter place. In the past week, Ralph had observed a

1:3 ratio in Sapp¡-Zapp! frequency, as well as an improvement of 12 bolts in the school's average Zapp! charge.

Ralph watched Joe Mode walking through Normal. Joe still had his cowboy hat and spurs, but he seldom reached for his six-guns anymore. As he said and did enZapping things—maintaining each person's self-esteem, listening to each person, and responding with empathy—little forks of lightning flashed between him and the others.

Things had improved, but the lightning still did not reach very far or last very long. When Joe was not around, people got dull quickly. Their glow faded, like red-hot steel cooling down and turning gray.

Most disappointing of all, very little Zapp! was getting to the students. They were no brighter than before. Unlike Zenith Elementary, Normal's Zapp! did not interconnect teachers and students, and the charge of energy never reached the threshold to become self-sustaining.

As Ralph was considering the situation, he felt a tremor in the floor. And a moment later another tremor. And another. Then from around the corner came the purple, scaly snout of the dragon.

Like all educational dragons, this one was invisible to the normal world, but its effects were quite real.

A swipe of its talons, and data in the Normal computer would be randomly trashed.

One switch of its tail, and a discipline problem would occur for Principal Joe.

A turn of its head, and a whole room full of students would become confused or bored.

Whenever this dragon breathed, crises broke out . . . problems with the air conditioning units, behavior problems galore, excessive absenteeism of students and teachers, the roof leaking in the gymnasium, science experiments not working, audiovisual equipment breaking down, students not doing their homework, and teachers failing to turn in reports.

The dragon squeezed its wings through the hallways of Normal Middle School, took a deep breath, and—whoosh—a long stream of red and orange arched across the school, igniting the school library, which burst into a tower of flames.

Joe, who had been in the middle of responding with empathy to something Phyllis had said, immediately broke off in mid-sentence and rushed to the fire, his cowboy hat bending and twisting as he hurried, until it became a white fireman's helmet.

Gladys, the librarian, who was closest to the conflagration, had already grabbed a 12th Dimension fire hose and was about to turn on the water, but Joe got there and wrestled it away from her.

Sapp¡—and Gladys' Zapp! charge, such as it was, was grounded.

"Stand aside!" yelled Joe. "Everybody out of the way!"

Joe stood there figuring out how to turn on the hose, while the flames rose higher.

Meanwhile, the dragon wandered down the hall

toward the office and flicked its long, forked tongue. The data disk in Mrs. Estello's word processor went up in smoke.

As usual, Mrs. Estello had no idea what to do. Her job was to be a secretary, and that was all. So, rather hurriedly, she took the smoking disk down the hall to Joe who, of course, was too busy wielding the fire hose to listen to her.

Sapp¡

So Mrs. Estello left the smoking disk beside Joe and headed for the faculty lounge for an aspirin. She talked to herself along the way.

The dragon roared again. More red and orange streaked through the air, and another fire erupted on the far side of the school, in the nurse's office. Then the dragon whipped its tail around to spread the flames.

Now three or four little fires were beginning to burn, and Joe was too busy fighting the first fire to notice them. Actually, he was too busy enjoying the challenge. It was fun being a fireman. In fact, he was not about to hand his hose or fireman's helmet over to anybody else. Why should he? Wasn't this his job?

He just about had the first fire doused when he saw the smoke from the others. All of a sudden, fire fighting wasn't so much fun. He tried rushing back and forth among them, spraying one, then the next. But as soon as he turned his back, the fires burned up and up and out of control.

Ralph watched, waiting for someone to help Joe,

but no one did. They were all thinking that Joe would know what to do. After all, it was his job. Joe might have given them little Zapps! now and then, but who were they to face dragons and raging fires? Against those problems, they were still just a bunch of Sapped zombies.

All but oblivious to Joe's heroics, they kept doing what they normally did, or just stood around and basked in the heat, while Joe ran from fire to fire. And Mrs. Estello, back from the faculty lounge, tagged along with her charred data disk, waiting for Joe to tell her what to do next.

The dragon grinned.

Ralph put in a call on the Ralphophone, but Joe, of course, was too busy to take it. Later, when Ralph came back to the normal world, they finally got together in Ralph's laboratory. Joe came in as sweaty and tired as a fireman could be—and more than a little impatient and frustrated.

"Ralph, this Zapp! stuff isn't working," he complained. "I have too many discipline problems in the school, the teacher certification report is late, and Superintendent Browning told me that the state's Standards Team might visit Normal soon. Also, we're behind with other reports in the office because Mrs. Estello doesn't have enough Zapp! to figure out what's wrong with her word processor disk."

Placing his hand on his forehead and sighing, Joe continued, "I'm too busy solving all the problems around Normal to Zapp anyone!"

Ralph, after some talking, persuaded Joe to go have

a look at what the dragon was doing in the 12th Dimension.

By the time they arrived, the dragon had had its fun. It had deposited a few eggs to hatch sometime later, incubated by the heat of smoldering fires, and had wandered on.

Most of the teachers, while showing concern about the dragon's fires, did very little, if anything. Why? Because they were accustomed to Principal Joe solving these problems. They just didn't feel any responsibility, because Joe had never given them responsibility.

In one classroom, a young teacher was wielding a fire hose and trying to organize a bucket brigade. But the Sapped students had very little interest in the buckets or in whether the fires were put out.

When the teacher was called away to hose down yet another fire, he neglected to tell the Sapped students to put the water *on the fire*. And since Sapped people can't think for themselves or make decisions on their own, the students splashed the water every which way. They were tripping over the buckets, spilling water, and bumping into one another. All of which was hysterical to the dragon.

Then, from down the hallway, came the siren. It was the administrative fire truck, gleefully driven by Mary Ellen Krabofski herself, trollish as ever, her fire engine-red fingernails curled around the steering wheel.

Riding the truck with her was the entire Central Office fire brigade. "Fire Expert" was printed in bright, gold letters on each of their slickers.

Mary Ellen brought the truck screeching to a halt and hopped out. The first thing she did was to run over and take the fire hose out of a teacher's hands.

"Gimme that," she yelled.

Sapp¡

And what did the expert fire fighters do? First, they ran around the truck half a dozen times, chasing everybody away.

Sapp¡ Sapp¡¡

Then *they* grabbed the buckets and started splashing water.

Sapp¡ Sapp¡¡ Sapp¡¡¡

Down the hall from where the fire truck had come, there now came a knight in shining armor on a white horse.

The knight rode up to Mary Ellen.

"Hi! I'm Sir Lancelot, a dragon specialist," he said. "I fight and kill dragons."

"About time you got here," she said.

"Wow, looks like you've got a big one," said the knight.

"We *know* that," said Mary Ellen, gesturing with the fire hose in hand. "Now go slay it, or I'll rust your armor."

Without even pausing to ask anyone where the dragon might be, the knight dropped his visor, lowered the point of his lance, and charged into the smoke. Unfortunately, his visibility was limited by the tiny slits in the visor, and the knight galloped right past the dragon, spearing two custodians instead.

Just then, the dragon slipped out the fire escape. It headed down the 12th Dimension path toward Zenith Elementary School, figuring to liven things up for the younger students.

Ralph and Joe followed at a discreet distance.

Of course, Zenith Elementary School was not exempt from visitations by monsters and education problems. Joe and Ralph arrived just after the dragon had entered a room where Cindy was holding a meeting with some teachers. As elsewhere, it huffed and puffed and breathed fire right into the middle of things.

But Cindy did not try to solve the problem of the dragon on her own. She did not put on armor and fight the dragon. She did not put on a fire helmet and fight the fire.

At the first whiff of smoke, she turned to the teacher nearest the fire hose and—lightning bolt forming in her hand—said, "We have a problem. I'd like your help. . . ."

Zapp!

And *that* teacher picked up the fire hose and figured out how to fight the fire—while Cindy pulled the others together into a group and said, "We have a big problem, and I'd like all of you to help. . . ."

Zapp! Zapp!!

The teachers then started talking among themselves about what to do, while Cindy checked on the fire. By the time she returned, the teachers had an action plan worked out.

At a nod from Cindy, some of them put on fire

helmets. Then Cindy got them some fire extinguishers, and they went to work on the new fires the dragon was starting.

The rest of the group put on armor and went to chase the dragon. Unlike many previous dragons, this one was too big for them to slay or tame on their own, but they did succeed in harassing it into leaving.

(All this did not take very long, because dragons, as you know, prefer dark and foggy places to lay their eggs, and there was too much energy and light in Zenith Elementary School for it to linger or lay many eggs.)

Meanwhile, Cindy had gone around to every other teacher in Zenith and said, "We're trying to solve a problem, and I'd like your help. . . ."

Zapp! Zapp!! Zapp!!!

The teachers filled in here and there for the others so that the regular work got done during the dragon crisis.

And after it was gone, it was clear that the dragon had not Sapped the school. With an abundance of Zapp!, it had been a lot like fighting fire with fire. In fact, the Zapp! now glowed even brighter than before, because people were charged up by having met the challenge.

Watching it all, Joe realized that Zapp! *did* work. He simply did not have enough of it in his school, and he was not using it fully yet.

Just as Joe and Ralph were about to leave, a knight on a large, white horse charged into the school. Cindy

Marks had to hurry over and grab the reins before he carelessly speared one of *her* staff members.

"Whoa!" she said. "May I help you with something?"

"Don't bother me. I'm on the trail of a big mother dragon," said the knight.

"It was here, but we chased it away," Cindy said.

"What?!" exclaimed the knight. "You dealt with it on your own? Impossible!"

"But we did," she said calmly.

Feeling threatened, the knight said, "Well, you can't do that. You're not allowed!"

Sapp¡

The knight rode away. But his Sapp¡ was soon overpowered by the Zapp! in Zenith Elementary School. No single Sapp¡ of a mere threatened knight could take away the energy they had achieved.

Joe and Ralph went back to Normal Middle School, where Joe called Phyllis, Mrs. Estello, and the other office staff together.

He began by saying, "I'd like your help in solving a problem."

Zapp!

JOE MODE'S NOTEBOOK

3rd principle of Zapp!

ASK FOR HELP
AND ENCOURAGE INVOLVEMENT

(Seek ideas, suggestions, and information)

18

In the next few days, Principal Joe spent most of his time getting Normal back to normal. Well, almost normal. During this time, his thoughts remained on Zapping, Sapping, and the dragon. "What had gone wrong?" he wondered.

So he called a faculty meeting for the upcoming afternoon. Joe started the meeting by asking, "So why are we having so many fires . . . excuse me . . . *problems* around here?"

At first, everyone was too Sapped to talk. After a minute of silence, Joe nearly threw his hands up and dismissed the meeting.

But instead, on a hunch, he used the first principle of Zapp! with the group. He told them that he knew they were all reasonable and smart people, that every day they saw what was going on, and that they probably had some good notions about what the problems were.

Susan was the first to venture a guess—with which Dolly promptly disagreed, putting forth a theory of her own. Then Dale had an idea, and before long, lots of people were talking.

Joe then Zapped some more by listening to what each person had to say. On a chalk board, he made a list of all their ideas about what might be happening.

They talked about each idea and then tried to decide on priorities. It was hard because there were a lot of problems at Normal. But finally, after a lot of voting, they chose the problem that should be attacked first: too many disruptions in the classrooms. Students were being taken from class for special services and extracurricular activities all the time. Everything, it seemed, came out of class time. The faculty decided they needed fewer disruptions and more time to teach.

"OK, thanks for your input," said Joe. "You're excused now."

Everybody nodded and walked away. But as they turned their backs, what happened in the 12th Dimension?

Sappi

Well, Joe Mode came up with a solution (and a brilliant one, he thought) to the problem of interruptions in the classroom. He prepared daily schedules for everyone, which reduced the number of disruptions by more than 50 percent.

Indeed, Joe's schedules did pretty much solve the interruption problem—when the teachers remembered the schedules and wanted to follow them. But the new schedules did not make life easier or more pleasant, especially for the special education teachers and the teachers with extracurricular assignments. In fact, nobody was very interested in whether the schedules were followed or not. Soon, new fires spread in the hallways and classrooms.

Joe talked to Ralph, for by now Joe had come to trust Ralph and his opinions.

"Ralph, why isn't my brilliant solution working?" he asked.

Ralph had a fairly good idea of what was wrong. Indeed, Joe had Zapped everyone by asking them to help him find the problem. Then Joe unintentionally Sapped them when he took the problem away from them and solved it himself.

"But they can't come up with solutions," argued Joe. "It'll be a waste of time. They don't have my experience, my administrative know-how, my grasp of the big picture."

"Oh?" challenged Ralph.

"Anyway, coming up with solutions is *my* job, isn't it?"

"Joe, the plain fact is that you still have fires out there," said Ralph. "Your idea might have been brilliant, but nobody else had a stake in making it work. They didn't own it. You did. It wasn't *their* solution."

Grumbling to himself, Joe finally admitted that Ralph might be right. He told Ralph to go have a look from the 12th Dimension while he talked with the teachers again. At this meeting, he asked for help not just in finding the problem, but in coming up with a solution.

It was Mary, the youngest special education teacher at Normal, who came up with the best idea. Less constrained by this-is-the-way-we-have-always-done-it thinking, she had a major insight.

Everyone, even a very surprised Joe Mode, knew immediately that her idea was great. The faculty talked in an excited way about its implications. There were Zapps all around.

"OK, thanks a lot for that great idea. I appreciate your help," Joe said. And then, with a wave good-bye, he added, *"I'll take it from here."*

As soon as he said that, Ralph, who was watching from the 12th Dimension, saw the lightning, which was glowing brightly among the people in the group, move from them to Joe. Once again Joe had taken their lightning—stolen it almost—and Sapp¡

Joe got busy and set up the procedures to implement their idea, but when he talked to the teachers about the changes each of them had to make, he could see that they were no longer enthusiastic. They just weren't very interested in whether the problem was solved or not. Or they said they didn't understand the new schedules. Or they privately came up with reasons why Joe's solution wouldn't work. Even though Joe had Zapped them in getting the idea, he had Sapped them by uninvolving them in implementing it.

Just then, in the 12th Dimension, the dragon was heard stomping down the school's driveway once more. It entered Normal Middle School and breathed fire all over the place. As usual, everyone stood around waiting for Joe to come and fight the fires. Which he did.

At the end of the day, having enjoyed itself immensely, the dragon wandered on.

Ralph challenged Joe and said, "You know, Joe, something isn't right."

"You're telling me!" said Joe.

"Don't you remember the very first time we saw Cindy Marks? Remember who fought the dragon?"

"It was one of the teachers," said Joe.

"That's right," said Ralph.

"And do you remember what happened when the new dragon showed up?"

"She got together a team to fight the dragon," said Joe.

"And do you remember who *did not* fight the dragon?"

"Well, sure," said Joe. "It was Cindy Marks who did not fight the dragon."

As soon as he said that, he understood. Cindy had offered help, but had not taken away from the individual or the group the challenge of fighting the dragon and its fires. She had left the responsibility with them.

At the next faculty meeting, Joe went over the interruption problem, and again the faculty discussed a solution. But after they had talked, Joe said, "Let's talk about what *you* need to make this work."

This time the Zapp! stayed with the people in the group. They owned the problem, the idea for solving it, *and* the challenge of making the idea succeed.

For a few of the teachers, this was too much too fast. After years of Sapp¡, suddenly having a bolt of lightning thrown at them was very frightening. Their immediate reaction was to try to get rid of it—to brush it off or throw the lightning back to Joe and the other teachers.

Joe had to react quickly to make sure these teachers did not Sapp¡ themselves. He listened to their fears and then said some things to maintain their self-esteem and build their confidence. He also instinctively lowered the voltage for these people, giving them smaller bolts of Zapp!, which would not blow their fuses.

Most of the teachers, though, were happy to accept the Zapp! They carried it away with them back to their classrooms, and it flashed and flickered among them even as they did their normal work.

By the time the dragon made its next rounds, everybody knew what to do as soon as its ugly head came around the corner. Rather than waiting for Joe to do something, they picked up the new fire hoses, armor, and swords they had asked Joe to purchase for them— and went after the dragon themselves.

Things were not perfect, mind you. Ray kept tripping over his hose. Dale busily dealt with a tiny fire, while behind him a huge one raged out of control. The dragon chasers were very clumsy with their weapons. And through the crisis, poor old Mrs. Estello just kept typing away, wondering what all the excitement was about.

But this day it was the teachers at Normal Middle

School who had the good time, not the dragon. The fires were put out very quickly. And the dragon soon left.

"We did it!" they all called to one another.

Watching what happened from the 12th Dimension, Ralph saw Normal light up like dawn. And that was how Joe Mode learned to generate the electric soul of Zapp! in the normal teachers at Normal.

JOE MODE'S NOTEBOOK

The Soul of Zapp!

OFFER HELP WITHOUT TAKING RESPONSIBILITY FOR ACTION

JOE MODE'S NOTEBOOK

The first three principles of Zapp! . . .

1. Maintain or Enhance Self-esteem.
2. Listen and Respond with Empathy.
3. Ask for Help and Encourage Involvement.

. . . lead to the Soul of Zapp!

OFFER HELP

WITHOUT TAKING

RESPONSIBILITY

FOR ACTION

19

As the school year went on, Joe Mode saw a lot more initiative and interest on the part of his teachers at Normal. The trouble was, these revved-up teachers were charging off in all different directions. There wasn't much of a focus.

The past crises had been exciting for the teachers. It had felt, well, kind of like fighting a pitched battle against an invisible dragon—and winning. Lots of the teachers secretly hoped that other problems would occur, and Joe found that some teachers were still working on old problems long after they had been solved.

Yes, Joe decided, they all needed some direction. And so he wrote in his notebook.

JOE MODE'S NOTEBOOK

- Zapp! does not guide action. It excites action.
- To get the job done, I have to channel the action in the right direction. But how?

Joe tried holding more faculty meetings so that everyone could talk about school improvements, but the meetings became another problem, not a solution. The meetings took a lot of extra time, and it seemed that every time Joe called a meeting, Mary Ellen Krabofski would just happen to stop by and wonder why none of the teachers were *teaching*.

Joe tried to explain to her that the meetings were important, but she didn't buy it.

"That's not what we're paying teachers to do," she complained.

Joe was stumped. How could he get the school—and the individual teachers—to do the right things without having a meeting every couple of days?

For a while, Joe let the teachers follow whatever initiatives they wanted to take. He thought it would increase their Zapp!

So when Luis came to him and said that he and some other teachers wanted to paint a mural on one of the walls, Joe said "OK" and helped them get the paint and brushes they needed.

The mural turned out well, and Luis and the other teachers received a lot of compliments.

So they decided to paint a few more murals, using their planning periods to do the work.

Joe began to wonder if the school really needed any more murals. But he did not want to Sapp¡ their initiative, so he said nothing.

Within a couple of weeks, Joe noticed that there were wall murals in almost every hall. They looked great. But he'd noticed something else: Discipline problems were creeping in, students seemed bored, and the teachers' rooms were a mess.

"That's strange," thought Joe.

Joe decided to walk over to the classrooms to talk with the teachers. But when he got there, he found two weeks' worth of work piled high on every teacher's desk.

"Hey, Luis, what's going on here?"

"No time," answered Luis. "We've all been too busy painting the murals."

"But painting murals isn't as important as teaching your students," said Joe.

"It isn't?" asked Luis.

"No, in fact, I'd say it's pretty low on the list of things you should be doing," said Joe.

Luis shook his head, dropped his brush in the paint can, and said, "Well, then, why didn't you *tell* us what was important so we wouldn't waste all this time?"

"Good question," Joe thought.

To make matters even worse, Ralph came in at the end of the day and reported that the school's Zapp! level was down 10 bolts, and dropping quickly. It seemed that without a dragon to focus their efforts on, teachers were changing things that didn't need to be changed, solving problems that didn't exist, throwing their energy in a thousand different directions, and Sapping themselves. Worst of all, they were Sapping the students.

Joe thought for a while. "There are so many things we need to accomplish. I don't know what's most important. Everything is important to someone!" he concluded. "Yet, the school needs direction."

Joe decided to ask for help. He went to Mary Ellen Krabofski to ask if she could offer advice and explain what the Central Office expected from him and his school.

But all Mary Ellen said was, "If you don't know what your job is, I'm not going to tell you."

Joe retreated to his office back at Normal. "If the Central Office can't give me direction," he thought, "then my teachers and I need to figure out what's important. We need to come up with goals for our school."

At a faculty meeting he asked, "What are the key

results we want to achieve, and how can we measure our success?" There was a lot of discussion.

Joe wrote down the top three *key result areas* they agreed on:

- Graduating students who are successful, productive, and happy later in life.
- Graduating students who know that learning is fun; that learning is a never-ending process.
- Pleasing the students' parents.

The next question they took up was *measurement*.

Soon it was obvious that some types of measurements would be easier than others. For example, it was easy to tell if the faculty had succeeded in teaching their students certain learning objectives: All they had to do was administer pre-tests and post-tests and then compare the results.

But just as quickly, they realized that other types of measurements would be more difficult.

How could the school measure whether it was teaching the right subjects to prepare students to be successful, productive, and happy? How could teachers tell whether the students were enjoying their classes, or whether the parents were pleased?

Joe and his teachers discovered that it was easier to figure out *what* they should be doing than it was to determine *how* they could measure their progress.

But the Normal principal and teachers refused to give up. In meeting after meeting, they wrestled with the challenge, considering each key result area and brainstorming possible methods of measurement.

Finally, they figured out that their first, most important key result area was too broad, and they rewrote it to say:

- Graduating students who do well academically, are active in extracurricular activities, and enjoy the high school experience.

They could track academic success once students moved on to Typical High School. They could also monitor the high school drop-out rate from year to year. The percentage of students entering college was another possible area of measurement. Another idea was to survey the students after their first year at Typical, to see whether they had found themselves prepared for high school.

But these measurements seemed very far off, and the teachers realized that they also needed to track intermediate accomplishments that related to each key result area. Student grades, criterion-referenced test performance, participation in extracurricular activities, homework completion, ability to write a research paper, and satisfaction with themselves and their school accomplishments were just a few of the areas they decided to monitor. They even decided that twice a year they would have students rate their classroom experiences, including teacher effectiveness.

And how would the faculty know if they were

successful? What was good performance? What would be their goals? Well, figuring that out took some time too. Some goals couldn't be set until baseline data was collected. But for most, they could make an educated guess with the intention of sharpening up the goals as they got used to the measurements.

After each meeting, Joe went to his notebook.

JOE MODE'S NOTEBOOK

To channel action, mutually establish the following:

Key Result Areas—the direction we want to go.

Measurements—ways to know we're moving in the right direction.

Goals—ways to tell us if we're there yet.

Just to be on the safe side (because he knew he might need some approvals from her later on), Joe ran all the school's key result areas, measurement methods, and goals past Mary Ellen Krabofski, who was actually quite impressed.

She immediately did some digging in her files and, from way in the back of her bottom drawer, produced a list of things Central Office's administration considered to be important to the district. This list had been created in a meeting several years ago, but nobody had done anything with the list—except to file it away.

As he looked over Mary Ellen's list, Joe was pleased to see that his teachers' ideas about what was important matched the Central Office's list in most areas. And where the lists differed, Joe now had some additional ideas to take back to his faculty.

At the next meeting, Joe shared the Central Office's list of priorities, and the group developed new key result areas where appropriate. Then they figured out ways to measure their progress in these areas, and they set goals for the current school year.

Then Joe suggested another idea he'd been considering: How about using the *school's* key result areas to develop key result areas, measurements, and goals *for each teacher?*

"How would that work?" asked Nancy.

"Each of you would have individual goals that would relate to the school's overall goals," answered Joe. "That way, you'd see how important you are to the overall success of the school."

"Great idea!" said several teachers. And they began working on individual plans for themselves.

What really got the teachers excited was the idea of *self*-measurement. All the teachers would be able to measure their own progress in different areas instead of having someone else measuring them. They decided that weekly measurements would be the best for most teachers, although some teachers—like the physical education instructors—preferred monthly progress checks.

Most everyone liked the idea, but the teachers often got stuck trying to come up with self-measurements.

Mrs. Schultz, a history teacher, realized that she needed to generate more student participation in her classes. Occasionally, she had tried to talk less, but she soon reverted to lecturing for most of every class. Now she was determined to increase the student participation rate, because she was sure that it would be related to the school's goals of student satisfaction and learning.

How could she measure her progress? She thought and thought, and finally came up with the idea of audiotaping one class per week. She could listen to the tape and determine what percentage of time she talked, and what percentage the students talked.

At the beginning, she talked 90 percent of the time, and the students 10 percent. But each week she improved, and eventually she got student participation up to 50 percent, which was her goal.

Joe knew that all his teachers felt proud of what they were accomplishing.

Now each teacher had personal goals . . . to help meet Normal's goals.

For the first time, the teachers knew what was important and why it was important. And they knew how they were doing relative to measurable goals.

That was an enormous Zapp!

Joe wrote in his notebook:

JOE MODE'S NOTEBOOK

Continued tracking of progress
toward goals creates Zapp!

The feedback from your boss
and others is helpful, but self-
measurement is best.

20

Time passed, and indeed things at Normal Middle School began to improve. One day, Joe was walking down the hall when Dale stopped him.

"How did the parent survey turn out?" asked Dale.

"Oh, OK," said Joe.

The next day a couple of other people asked, "Say, Joe, how's the school doing?"

"Pretty well," said Joe.

After that, they quit asking. A few days later, Joe noticed that there seemed to be a slacking off of improvement efforts. Ralph had been taking his own measurements of the Zapp! levels, and he too had found that they were indeed falling off.

"I told them they were doing pretty well. What's going on?" Joe asked Ralph.

"But what does *pretty well* mean?" Ralph chided. "Joe, if you were a basketball player, how good could you be if you could never see whether the ball went into the basket? Or what if you had to play every day, but no one would tell you the score? People who are involved in their work want to know exactly how the whole team is doing—and not tomorrow, today."

"I see what you mean," said Joe.

By the next afternoon, there were graphs on the walls of the teachers' lounge, showing the progress toward each of the school's goals. Next to the school's goals, Joe had left room for individual teachers' progress toward their goals, which supported the overall goals.

Joe encouraged the teachers to post their own progress charts and to keep them up to date. Most of the teachers posted their charts in the lounge, but some decided to share their goals with their students, so they posted them in the classrooms.

Sharing the measurement methods and goals had an amazing effect. Teachers started helping each other— sharing "tricks of the trade" learned through experience. They took great pride in one another's accomplishments, and they were supportive when there was a temporary downturn in the data.

Because they could see what their fellow teachers were trying to accomplish, there was more cooperation around the school.

Students quickly picked up on the idea of setting and tracking goals. Knowing the teachers' goals made the students feel trusted, and they responded by helping the teachers reach their goals. For example, Mrs. Schultz, the history teacher, found that her students became more participative after they learned about her goal for her classes.

What Joe hadn't expected was that students wanted to set their own goals and chart their own progress. In the gym classes, for example, students were charting things like strength, endurance, and agility. This really excited the students, and the Zapp! level continued to increase.

"Why shouldn't students share the responsibility of setting the school's goals," thought Joe, and he tried the idea out—first with a few classes, and then with all the Normal students. He placed student representatives on committees to set goals and review progress. He set up committees to define measurement methods, and he announced goals in the student newspaper. Gradually, more and more students became involved.

Along with student involvement came an increased interest in the school's progress. The charts showing the school's progress toward goals were moved out of the teachers' lounge and into the hallway so all the students could see how things were going. Students were particularly interested in the data on student success at Typical High School, and they quickly figured out how achievement of Normal goals would contribute to their later success.

Students learned that their class goals needed to be part of the school's goals, and they took on their new challenge with enthusiasm. This led to a lot more participation in school activities and more support of one another. Student learning teams sprouted up. The teachers and students began to take responsibility for one another's progress.

Despite Joe's fears, he discovered that sometimes bad news could be a Zapp! How could that be? Because people tried a little harder if they saw they were falling behind.

And if someone continued to fall behind, nobody had to be the bad guy in saying something about performance being off. The measurements told the story.

In the middle of the year, a tragedy struck Normal School District. A high school student who had just received his driver's license ran off the road and into a ravine. The driver was killed instantly. His companion, a student at Normal, would never be able to walk again. Tests had shown that both students had had high blood alcohol levels at the time of the accident.

The tragic accident forced the schools to recognize what many already knew: The use of drugs and alcohol by students was increasing. Everyone at Normal wanted to do something, so the teachers and Joe decided to set up a new key result area to address this problem.

The challenge was to develop appropriate measurement methods. With a great deal of participation from students, the teachers came up with creative ideas. They decided to measure the percentage of students signing "contracts" not to use drugs, as well as the percentage of families agreeing not to serve alcohol at student parties held in their homes.

To help educate students and parents, the teachers developed a booklet on "facts and fantasies" about drugs and alcohol. Finally, an anonymous survey was developed to provide the school with baseline data about students' use of drugs and alcohol, with subsequent surveys planned to determine the success of various interventions. These goals galvanized the school toward meaningful action.

Now, real progress could be seen and measured. From this experience, Joe learned an important lesson: You can change people's focus by changing what you measure. This was so important that Joe decided to make an entry in his notebook.

JOE MODE'S NOTEBOOK

Managing by Measurement:

- Continuous tracking of progress toward goals keeps the Zapp! level high.
- Teachers should track their own progress toward goals.
- Whenever possible, students should track their own progress toward goals.
- Changing measurements and goals Zapps people in new directions.
- One of the most effective things a school leader can do is change the measurements to reflect what is most important.

Most of the time, the measurements on the graphs went up, up, up. And by the end of the school year, Normal was reaching or exceeding most of its goals.

Things were going well for Joe and Normal Middle School. At the last regularly scheduled faculty meeting of the year, Joe commended all the teachers on their progress. In fact, this was more of a celebration than a meeting. Joe wanted the teachers to know how proud he was of their hard work and success.

What about the students? "Ah," thought Joe and the teachers. "Let's hold a party!" So they did. It didn't take much effort to get the students involved and interested. They quickly set a date, arranged for refreshments and activities, and decided that they all wanted some memento of the school's achievements.

Some of the woodworking students suggested a three-inch wooden version of the number "1" with the school's name painted on it. It was a good idea, but would require a lot of hard work.

Student teams committed to cutting out the figures, sanding the wood, and painting them. Many students were involved, because time was short. But the job was accomplished, the party was held, and everyone was very proud of their new symbol.

Perhaps Normal wasn't yet really and truly number one but, to them, they were number one. And they were proud of it.

21

When the new school year started, Normal Middle School really began to experience the power of Zapp! In addition to raising the targets in many of the past year's key result areas, the teachers and students decided to tackle a new—and really tough—problem: handling students with special needs who, because of mainstreaming, were increasingly represented in most classes.

Both teachers and students needed more knowledge and training about understanding different needs and helping students value diversity in their school environment. Student committees, teacher committees, and parent committees were set up. And systems were established so that the committees could meet frequently with each other to share insights and communicate efforts.

Teachers began to feel the lightning in their teaching. Students began to feel the lightning in their learning.

And how did Joe Mode feel? Did he feel like a hero? Did he feel terrific?

No, he began to feel more and more nervous and scared.

Ralph noticed the change.

"Joe, what's wrong?" he asked. "You look worried. You're not Zapping people the way you could be. What's holding you back?"

Joe muttered some feeble excuses, but Ralph kept pressing him until he admitted what was really bothering him.

"To Zapp people in a big way, I have to encourage them to get involved and take responsibility, right?" asked Joe.

"Right."

"But if I let other people take responsibility, how do I know they'll live up to it?"

"Beats me. I guess you have to trust them," offered Ralph.

"Trust them? That's easy for you to say. Remember when I tried letting everybody make his or her own decisions? It was a disaster!" said Joe.

"That's true," Ralph agreed.

"So how can I control what's going on?" asked Joe. "What if nothing gets done on time? What if somebody does something I don't know about and everything gets messed up? Who is Mary Ellen Krabofski going to yell at?"

"You," admitted Ralph.

"Right. Me. I'll get yelled at. I'll get the blame. And if the mistake is bad enough, there's no telling what could happen to me," said Joe. "Sure, I'd like people to be Zapped—but not if it's going to get me in trouble."

"Look, you Zapped me when you asked for help figuring out how Cindy ran Zenith Elementary School. You gave me responsibility. Did I let you down?" Ralph argued.

"No, but I knew what you were doing," said Joe.

"Well?"

Had you been in the 12th Dimension, you would have seen a new sun rise inside Joe's head. Of course! Offering help to people in the school in part meant staying in touch with them, knowing what they were doing and what they planned to do, keeping them on track.

In short, there still had to be some sort of control and coordination. But how could he keep track of people's activities without Sapping everyone?

Within five minutes, Joe had everything he needed to figure it out.

The phone rang, and it was a new student teacher who was having trouble with one of her students. Debra felt comfortable *teaching,* but she was very uncomfortable *disciplining*.

Joe thought back to his student-teacher days a long time ago. He had been unsure about handling discipline problems too, but now it was a routine part of his job.

"How about if I role-play the situation with you before you meet with the boy? That will give you some practice, and maybe I'll be able to give you a few pointers," offered Joe.

"That would be great," said Debra, relieved. "In fact, that's just what I need—a good coach!"

All of a sudden, the bells went off in Joe's head. Of course! Debra needed more of Joe's help because she was new to teaching. She needed more coaching and more frequent checks than an experienced teacher.

And that's when it hit him: Control, in the sense of knowing what's going on, didn't have to be a Sapp¡ It could be a Zapp! It all depended on the situation and the person.

Joe figured out that control was largely a matter of how often he should check on how his teachers were doing and how he did the checking. Repeated coaching and checking up on experienced teachers would be a Sapp¡ and a waste of time. But coaching and checking up on a new teacher, or a teacher experiencing difficulties, would be a Zapp! because it showed concern— and this certainly would be an excellent use of a principal's time.

Joe also learned that there were many different ways of knowing what was going on. Of course, classroom observation was important, as were periodic written reports on progress and one-on-one meetings with teachers. But far less threatening were "management by exception" controls. People were told that they needed to inform the principal only when measurements passed a prearranged trigger point—like the time cafeteria usage went down three months in a row, and Joe felt the need for more information.

Most importantly, Joe discovered an extremely effective control was just to walk around and talk with people. This way, he found out what was going on, and he had the opportunity to throw a few Zapps! into the conversation.

It took some practice, but Joe finally got the hang of it. He learned that instead of looking over everyone's shoulder, he could help teachers *as they needed it.*

JOE MODE'S NOTEBOOK

A school leader needs to know what's going on in the school—with the students, teachers, and support staff. Observations, periodic written reports, and meetings are effective methods of leader control—but so is just walking around.

The best way of knowing what's going on is to coach people.

- A principal who *over*controls Sapps.
- A principal who *abandons* control Sapps.
- A principal who uses *situational* control Zapps.

People respond negatively to controls only when they are inappropriate for the situation.

Through practice, Joe also learned that he could share responsibility with his faculty without the teachers thinking he was abandoning them. Through Zapp!, teachers and staff took on new responsibilities, and that was good.

Joe could see that his role was changing, but it was as important as ever.

He went to his notebook.

JOE MODE'S NOTEBOOK

My role as a school leader is changing. But I still have the responsibility to:

- Know what is going on.
- Establish direction for the school.
- Ensure that the teachers and staff are on course.
- Make the decisions that the teachers can't.
- Offer a guiding hand and open doors to clear the way.
- Help to assess performance.
- Be a smart principal . . . and a good coach.

22

Unfortunately, Mrs. Estello was still making mistake after mistake with hardly a break.

One day Joe went over to her and pointed out this fact. He tried to be as patient as he could as he said, "You see, the problem is that for the school to reach its new goals, we're going to need your help in reducing the number of mistakes in the work coming from your area."

Mrs. Estello nodded vaguely and looked as if she might be thinking about an unpleasant side effect of something she'd eaten for lunch.

"You've been doing this job for a long time," Joe continued. "I'm sure that with all your experience, you can think of ways you might improve your accuracy."

"I can?" she asked.

"Sure you can! Just give it a try. We'll talk about it on Wednesday, and if there are things you need, let me know," said Joe.

He went away thinking that surely Mrs. Estello would respond to what he had said.

Yet, two days later, Mrs. Estello was still making all

kinds of blunders. On Tuesday, 20 cases of flour had arrived at the cafeteria, when the dieticians had asked for 20 cartons of vegetables—all because Mrs. Estello had hit the wrong code key on her computer and never looked back.

Just about everything coming from her had to be done over again, and by Wednesday her performance had gotten worse instead of better. Teachers' complaints to Joe about Mrs. Estello's work were increasing.

Joe talked with Mrs. Estello again.

"Why do you think you're making so many mistakes?" he asked.

"I don't know," she said.

"How could you improve?"

"I don't know."

"Didn't you come up with any ideas like we talked about?" Joe asked.

"Not yet. I haven't had time," said Mrs. Estello.

After school that evening, Joe was telling his wife, Mabel Mode, what had happened.

"She's hopeless! She'll never get it! Never in a billion years!" Joe complained to Mabel.

"Maybe you're asking too much too soon from Mrs. Estello," Mabel suggested.

"But she's holding back the whole school!" Joe cried. "I should fire her!"

"Now, now," said Mabel. "Why don't you go out in the backyard, cool down, and see what the kids are up to."

Joe figured that was a good idea. He needed some time to think.

When he got outside, he found their young son, Jack, and their daughter, Jill, learning how to play baseball. He watched as little Jack Mode flailed away at the ball his older sister was pitching.

After his fourth useless swing, little Jack turned and said, "Dad, I can't do it!"

"Sure you can," said Joe.

"But I don't know how!"

So Joe stepped down from the porch and worked with little Jack.

First, Joe talked with little Jack to make sure he understood the object of the game. Then they talked about important details: how Jack had to keep his eye on the ball, when to swing, and how to choke up on the bat to get more control.

Next, Joe said, "Now watch me." And he took the bat and showed little Jack how it was done.

Then he gave the bat back to Jack and said, "Here, you try it now."

Which Jack did. The ball came across the rock they were using for home plate, and little Jack swung the bat—and missed.

But, being a good father, Joe did not yell at him. He just said, "Good swing! Now try it again. You'll get the hang of it. Remember, keep your eye on the ball."

Then he had Jack practice—over and over again.

Finally—CRACK!—little Jack connected and sent the ball rocketing over the back hedge.

"See, you're a natural!" called Joe, as his son ran for the brick that represented first base.

Of course, little Jack was *not* a natural baseball player. He had succeeded because his father had taken the time to coach him and because he had practiced. And, as Joe watched proudly while little Jack ran the bases, he suddenly realized that this is what he had to do with Mrs. Estello.

He had to be a coach.

Just as he would never tell his kids, "If you don't hit the ball the first time, you're out of the family," it wasn't right for him to demand too much of Mrs. Estello without helping her to live up to his expectations.

The next day, Joe approached Mrs. Estello and said, "Mrs. Estello, I'm going to work with you on this. Maybe if we put our heads together, we can figure this out. Now first, let's talk about what we're trying to accomplish. . . ."

By and by—working not only with Mrs. Estello, but with others as well—Joe found that there were seven basic steps to being a good coach on the job.

First, he had to establish the overall purpose of the task and explain why it was important—how it related to achieving the school's goals or the individual's goals.

Then he had to explain the process (the steps) to be used in accomplishing the task.

Next, he had to demonstrate how the process was done or have someone else provide a demonstration.

Then Joe had to observe while the person practiced the process.

He had to provide immediate and specific feedback, and coach again or reinforce success.

Joe had to express confidence in the person's ability to continue to accomplish the task successfully.

And finally, they had to agree on the follow-up actions—in other words, how they would measure progress.

JOE MODE'S NOTEBOOK

To get maximum Zapp!, many people need coaching on how to do their jobs.

Coaching steps:

1. Explain the purpose and importance of what you are trying to teach.
2. Explain the process (the steps) to be used.
3. Show how it's done (model the behavior).
4. Observe while the person practices the process.
5. Provide immediate and specific feedback (coach again or reinforce success).
6. Express confidence in the person's ability to be successful at the task.
7. Agree on follow-up actions.

For example, through coaching, Joe tried to keep Mrs. Estello from making mistakes in the first place. When a new project was assigned, he coached her so she would *start out* doing it correctly.

Joe found that Mrs. Estello learned much faster when he coached her before the start of a project instead of after she had made some mistakes. That way, Mrs. Estello never had a chance to learn bad habits or get frustrated by the mistakes she was making. Coaching made a new project exciting and challenging.

Most of all, coaching gave Mrs. Estello the confidence to try new tasks, like using a new computer program recommended by the Central Office. Joe learned that it wasn't a lack of ability holding her back from trying new things nearly as much as it was a lack of confidence in herself. Her successes built confidence, which led to more successes, which led to more confidence.

Zapp!

JOE MODE'S NOTEBOOK

People learn faster from successes than from failures.

It still took time for Mrs. Estello to improve, but she did. (In the meantime, Joe asked the other staff members dealing with her to come up with some ways to lighten her load, which they did.)

One of the problems Joe discovered was that very little of the information Mrs. Estello was processing was meaningful to her. What required immediate attention and what didn't? What made sense and what didn't? She did not know.

So Joe took her into his office and explained to her what was what. Then he chose some of her most common reports and arranged for her to talk with the people who needed these reports. She found out how the data was used and why it was important. During this process, she even found that one report she'd been spending an entire day every month to complete wasn't used anymore—so she stopped producing it.

Joe also allowed her time to talk with teachers about their expectations for the school's secretary. Little by little, he expanded Mrs. Estello's universe.

Zapp!

JOE MODE'S NOTEBOOK

Learning more about your job boosts your Zapp!

When Mrs. Estello did something wrong, Joe would take her aside and explain what was wrong and show her how to correct the problem. Every time Mrs. Estello did something right, Joe made sure she knew about it. He told her why it was right and talked to her about what she had to do to *keep* getting it right.

Zapp!

Still, it was not a steady climb for Mrs. Estello. From time to time, she would get angry at Joe for asking her to do things that she didn't want to do. Or she would become defensive about her performance. Or she would get the idea that Joe was manipulating her, and her trust in him would weaken. And then she would slip back into her old ways and attitudes.

When that happened, Joe relied upon the key principles he had learned to get her back on an upward path again. He did this by maintaining her self-esteem, listening and responding with empathy, asking for her help in solving problems, and offering help without taking responsibility away from her.

Sure enough, Mrs. Estello would begin to improve again.

And it was working with other people too.

Zapp!

JOE MODE'S NOTEBOOK

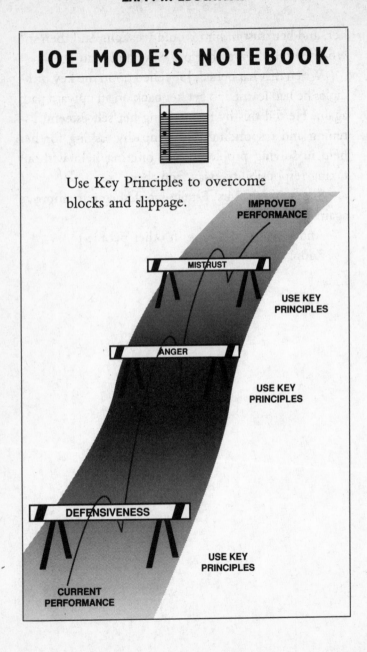

Use Key Principles to overcome blocks and slippage.

IMPROVED PERFORMANCE

MISTRUST

USE KEY PRINCIPLES

ANGER

USE KEY PRINCIPLES

DEFENSIVENESS

USE KEY PRINCIPLES

CURRENT PERFORMANCE

Later on, Joe got Mrs. Estello some help in learning to spot the problems she was having, analyze them, and come up with solutions.

Zapp!

Then Mrs. Estello *herself* asked for some additional training to learn more about using her computer.

Zapp!!

Based on her training, Mrs. Estello learned how to set up her keyboard so that she could create a whole paragraph just by hitting one key. And she asked Joe for a software program to check her spelling. She wanted to be *accurate!*

Zapp!!!

Then she figured out how she could type an entire form by selecting from half a dozen keys that filled in the blanks automatically.

Zapp!!!!

And before long, Mrs. Estello was not hopeless. She was good at what she did.

She was a fully glowing member of Normal's team.

23

Month after month, Joe could see that not only was the school changing, but his principal's role was changing as well. He was no longer the principal he used to be.

For years, Joe had believed that he knew just about everything there was to know about being a principal. In his own mind, he had seen himself as a lieutenant in the Army of Education.

To be a good lieutenant, he was supposed to:

Follow orders from above,
Make all the decisions for his "troops,"
Keep everyone under control,
Be hard and unapproachable,
Bark orders at people, and
Yell at people who did something wrong.

Hadn't that worked for John Wayne in all those war movies? Yet it no longer worked, if it ever really had, at Normal Middle School. Something had long been missing.

What he had learned was that his position required him to be less like a tough principal and more like a good parent. When Joe was growing up, his parents had helped him grow from a helpless kid to a responsible member of the family. Slowly they involved little Joe and his brothers and sisters in running the household. They gave them more and more responsibility and decision-making power as they grew up.

Of course, Joe knew that his teachers were adults and not kids, but he knew that the same ideas—growth, involvement, increasing freedom with increasing responsibility—applied to adults too.

His principal's job was no longer a matter of ordering teachers around. His job was to supply what the faculty needed in order to grow in their teaching professions and to be successful.

And what was it that Zapped people needed?

First, teachers needed *direction*. It was Joe's job to make sure his staff worked on the right things. He did this by establishing key result areas, measurements, and goals.

Second, teachers needed various types of *knowledge and skills*. For example, they needed advanced instructional training to bring out the best in every student, personal skills such as time management, and an understanding of how the entire system operates.

Third, teachers needed the principal to give them the necessary *resources*—equipment, materials, facilities, time, and money.

Fourth, teachers needed Joe's *support*—encouragement, authorization, coaching, feedback, recognition, and reinforcement.

Instead of trying to be the solitary "hero," Joe Mode—like Cindy Marks—was giving staff members whatever was required to let each of *them* be the "hero." He gave whatever was needed, and they gave back their personal best.

JOE MODE'S NOTEBOOK

For Zapp! to work, people need:

- Direction (key result areas, goals, and measurements).
- Knowledge and skills (advanced training, self-management, and an understanding of how the system operates).
- Resources (equipment, materials, facilities, time, and money).
- Support (encouragement, authorization, coaching, feedback, recognition, and reinforcement).

All this was fine with Joe. He liked his position better this way, and his teachers seemed to like their assignments better. Yet, something was bothering him.

One evening he told Mabel, "You know, I don't seem like a *principal* anymore. The title doesn't fit. I'm not *looking over* people now."

"So what do you do in your job now?" Mabel asked.

"Well, I point out to the faculty and staff which direction we have to go in, and I guide them so they get there on their own, but with no one straying too far off the path. That way, we all get there together," explained Joe.

"To me," said Mabel, "that sounds like the job of a leader. You're not directing as much as you're leading a group."

"To lead the group," Joe thought, *"rather than direct the group."*

He sat back and tried to imagine his name linked to a new title:

Joe Mode
School Leader

"Hmmm," he mused. "I kind of like that."

And the Zapp! grew.

Joe was walking around Normal Middle School one afternoon when he passed Debra, who told him about a discipline problem she had encountered that morning. But Joe was not to worry about it, for it was not a problem anymore—because Debra had already handled it on her own.

Then, as Joe passed Jenny's room, he stopped in to say hello. Jenny was in the middle of the room working with Sarah, a slow learner. Because Sarah was falling behind in her classes, Jenny had been using her planning period to tutor her. Jenny beamed as she told Joe how much improvement Sarah was making in her classes. Not only was Sarah doing better in school, but she was becoming more confident. In fact, she had even signed up for her first after-school activity. It was obvious that Jenny was proud of Sarah. Sarah smiled, and Joe felt good as he left the room.

Walking down Corridor B, Joe spotted Ralph, who was talking with two other teachers about revising the science curriculum guide.

As Joe passed a group of students, they all smiled and spoke to him. They were happy, and Joe felt good, because all was *not* normal at Normal. It was much better.

Just then Phyllis hurried by and nodded to Joe. She had just completed a grant application for the school and wanted to get it in the mail right away. As she passed him, Phyllis suggested that Joe should stop by to see the students who were practicing for the school play.

Upon entering the auditorium, Joe observed Amy, a third-year language arts teacher, directing play practice for some of her students. Amy was especially helpful to Kristin, a blind student. When Kristin had said that she'd like to participate in the play, Amy and the other students had decided it would be a great experience for Kristin. They were all working hard—especially Kristin!—to make sure her lines and movements were just right.

Down the hall, Dolly came out of her classroom to tell Joe that the Normal cheerleaders had just won an award for sportsmanship and enthusiasm. Joe smiled and thought, "Maybe Normal Middle School should have been called Great Middle School because now we seem to be great."

As Joe entered the secretary's area, he was again impressed. Mrs. Estello, now the master of her computer, was driving that machine as fast as it would go, and having more fun than in all her other 30 years at Normal put together.

Joe looked around, amazed. Normal people were acting like owners of their work, and they were proud of what they did. Things were not perfect, and probably never would be. But they were a lot better, and sometimes they were fantastic. Normal people had a sense of who they were, they liked it, and they knew where they were headed.

Joe was pleased with what he had heard and seen. As he went into his office, he thought about his new role as leader. Indeed, he felt like a *leader*!

In his office, Joe relaxed and remembered that it had been a long time since he had seen what all this looked like in the 12th Dimension. He suspected things would look different from what he remembered, so he decided to find Ralph and hitch a ride on the Ralpholator.

When Joe got to Ralph's lab, all was quiet. Ralph was not there, but a note on his door read:

GONE TO 12TH
BE BACK SOON

Joe decided to join Ralph in the 12th Dimension. So he sat down in the chair by the Ralpholator. By now, Ralph had installed menu-driven software for the Ralpholator, making it easy for Joe to figure out which commands to enter.

He double-clicked the computer mouse. There was a high-pitched whine, a blinding flash, and then Joe Mode vanished.

When he opened his eyes, Joe saw Normal Middle School in a light in which he had never seen it before. The fog had lifted. As he walked around, it was as if the sun had come out, except that the sun was inside the teachers, the staff, and the students.

In the shadowy corners, there were still some dragon eggs, and nothing could be done at the moment to dislodge them. But Joe remembered when all he saw were walls of stone, glass, and steel.

Well, the stone walls were tumbling and crumbling. The glass walls had been vaporized. And the Zapp! had melted holes in the steel walls, forming doors.

As Joe looked around, he saw no more zombies, no more mummies, no more headless giants.

Everybody at Normal was growing into exactly what they were—*human beings*.

Joe was extremely happy with what he saw.

But Ralph was nowhere to be seen, and Joe wanted to talk to him.

Joe decided to see if Ralph might be at Zenith Elementary School. He left the bright, lightning lights of Normal and found his way through the still-foggy buildings in the rest of Normal School District.

He passed the mother dragon, who was wreaking havoc at Typical High School but who, oddly enough, seemed a bit smaller than when he had seen her last.

He passed more dragon eggs, swarms of zombies, and lots of other strange sights. Finally, he arrived at Zenith Elementary School.

Much to his satisfaction, Joe saw that the Zapp! of his own school was now about the same as Zenith Elementary's.

But where was Ralph? Not at Zenith. So Joe went back into the fog and checked a few more places, but Ralph was not in any of his usual haunts.

As he kept looking, Joe roamed farther and farther through the fog. Pretty soon, Joe gave up, but when he tried to go back, he realized he was lost.

For a while, he wandered around haphazardly. He happened down a winding staircase, through a courtyard, and into a wide archway flanked by a massive set of gates, where a bored security guard stood leaning on his 12th Dimension spear.

On the far side of the archway, Joe realized that he was *outside*. In fact, he was standing on the planks of what he came to realize was a drawbridge. When Joe turned around and looked up at the Normal Central Office building as it appeared in the 12th Dimension, he saw something like a castle.

And there, standing in front of him on the far side of the moat, were Ralph Rosco and Cindy Marks.

"Hi, Joe," called Ralph.

"Pretty wild, isn't it?" said Cindy, smiling.

"What are you two doing here?" asked Joe.

"Ralph has been showing me around," said Cindy. "In fact, we were watching you for a while. I was picking up a few pointers."

"You were?" asked Joe, smiling sheepishly.

"I think it's time we compared notes, don't you?" asked Cindy.

And they did just that.

PART III

Super-charged Zapp!

24

As experts on the subject now agree, there are two ways to enter the 12th Dimension. The first is by sitting in the swivel chair wired to Ralph Rosco's Ralphola-tor. The second is to bump into someone by accident who is already in the 12th Dimension.

Which was what Cindy Marks had done.

Ralph (invisible, of course) had been in the 12th Dimension, with Zappometer in hand, as he wandered over to Zenith Elementary School to have a look at a new kind of lightning he had noticed.

Cindy had been hurrying toward her desk to take a phone call when Zapp!—she slammed right into him, was drawn into his field, and vanished from the normal world of three dimensions.

When her eyes adjusted, she found herself in the land of lightning bolts and strange-yet-brilliant visions. And here was this guy saying, "Oh, hi, remember me? Gee, I guess you'd like to know where you are and what's going on, wouldn't you?"

"Yes, please," said Cindy, hands covering her pounding heart.

So Ralph calmly reintroduced himself and gave her the grand tour. That was what they were doing when Joe Mode showed up.

Well, once she heard what had been going on, Cindy could have been a little upset that Joe had not gone to her and been more open about things. But Cindy was more interested in this new way of looking at how the different schools in the district *really* operated, and she was even *more* fascinated by the power of Zapp!

"All these years I've been trying to create this, without ever knowing if it really existed," she said. "And now I can actually see it!"

"But what are you doing out *here*?" Joe asked them.

"It occurred to me as I was showing Cindy around," answered Ralph, "that I had never looked at the whole district from the perspective of the 12th Dimension. So we came out here to take a look."

They all turned toward the big, stony, dour, gray shape behind them. Actually, it was not so much like one huge castle as it was a huge cluster of smaller ones. A maze of walls, towers, and parapets. Little fortresses joined by common walls. Battlements that went up and up toward the sky, layer upon layer, much like a pyramid.

Lo and behold, before them stood the entire Normal School District in a condensed sort of way. Actually, it looked a lot like the organization chart developed by the Board of Education. In the center, rising from the uppermost tier of the highest battlements was the tallest tower, from which flew the Normal Central Office flag. And there, in a balcony alcove of that tallest tower, was the superintendent of Normal School District, Dr. Browning, who was drinking a cup of coffee as he studied the prepared agenda for an upcoming Board of Education meeting.

"But where is Normal Middle School?" asked Joe, who wanted to know (as Cindy had before he had arrived) where his own school stood in the scheme of things.

"It's over there. Don't you see it?" asked Ralph, pointing to one of the smaller towers on the outer battlements.

Joe finally saw which tower Ralph was pointing to. It was the one with the glow of lightning bolts behind its windows.

Then Joe noticed that unlike the other towers of the school district castle, which typically had narrow, rectangular windows, this tower—their tower—had little *round* windows.

And *fins*.

It also had a smoother, sleeker shape than the other towers.

This tower seemed to be much more *fluid* somehow.

As Joe scanned the sight before him, there, on the far side of the outer battlements, was another tower, also with fins and little round windows. And behind the windows, the lightning of Zapp! flickered and glowed.

It was, of course, Zenith Elementary School.

Whatever these new towers were, they were different from the others. Something very extraordinary was taking place.

Joe could see that they were no longer shapes of set stone, but shapes transforming, evolving into something new.

25

Well, they all found it very interesting to see the district this way, but it was time to get back to their schools. So the three of them returned to the worlds of Normal and Zenith. In parting, there were lots of promises to talk often and keep in touch.

But those promises were never kept.

In days to come, they were all much too busy with their own schools.

Cindy Marks did visit Normal a couple of times, and she asked to use the Ralpholator so that she could do some exploring on her own.

And then lots of people from Zenith Elementary School took a field trip to the 12th Dimension. Not just teachers, but parents and students as well.

This miffed Joe Mode a bit. People coming in and out were a bit disruptive, and they were making demands on Ralph's time.

But this was a minor irritation. Joe Mode had lots of other things to keep him occupied. Chief among them was the task of trying to keep everyone Zapped.

One afternoon on his way home, Joe finally admitted something to himself that he really didn't want to: As time went on, he was finding it harder—not easier—to keep the teachers, the staff, and the students Zapped.

Joe was using everything he knew, but he could not get the kind of quantum improvement in involvement and performance that he had been getting before. Zapp! as he would, Joe even found the overall lightning level falling off just a little. And he knew it even without Ralph telling him the exact measurements.

"What else can I do?" Joe asked himself as he drove home. Then he shrugged and said, "Well, maybe we've reached our zenith. Maybe this is as good as it gets."

About a week later, Ralph came into Joe's office with a copy of *The Horace Mann News* and asked, "Hey, Joe, have you seen this?"

On the front page was a story that read:

ZENITH ELEMENTARY SCHOOL RECEIVES RECOGNITION AND GRANT FOR EXCELLENCE IN EDUCATION

Assistant Superintendent Mary Ellen Krabofski congratulated Zenith Elementary's principal, Cindy Marks, and her teachers and staff members for being named a School of Excellence. Also, the Better Schools Foundation awarded the school $150,000 to develop a Math and Science Center for teachers and students.

"The school-based Diamond Team deserves all the credit," said Cindy Marks. "Their hard work, enthusiasm, and creativity are what allowed us to overcome many fathomless pitfalls in our path and enrich the quality of education at our school. I'm quite proud of our Zenith students, teachers, staff, and parents."

"An award and a grant?! What's going on over there?" asked Joe.

"I don't know," said Ralph. "I figured we were doing as well as they were, so I haven't been checking on them lately."

"Fire up that machine of yours, and let's go find out what they're doing," said Joe.

When they got to Zenith Elementary School in the 12th Dimension, everything looked about the same as usual. Cindy was walking around in her wizard hat, and the usual miraculous things were going on. But then Ralph started getting a very strong reading on his Zappometer.

"Look at this, Joe. Zenith Elementary is running at 100 bolts an hour!" said Ralph. "The best we've ever done is 75."

"How could that be?" asked Joe. "We were the same just a little while ago."

"What can I say?" asked Ralph. "The Zappometer does not lie."

Just then Ralph saw the new, strange kind of lightning he had noticed the day Cindy Marks had bumped into him. It came from a group of students who were working in the conference area.

Joe and Ralph moved closer to the new lightning and, as they did, the Zappometer went off the scale.

But they didn't need an instrument to tell them they were seeing something different from the usual Zapp! they were accustomed to seeing.

Because this was a *wheel* of lightning.

There was the student team working on the gem-encrusted mountain. The hot-air balloon that the students had first used to cross the chasm hung limply from a rocky ledge, discarded on the other side and swaying in the 12th Dimension breeze. The team no longer needed the balloon because the students had built a bridge across the chasm.

This wheel of Zapp! ran round and round among them, both directions at once, and back and forth over the diameter of the group as the students worked.

The kind of Zapp! that Ralph and Joe had been used to seeing in the 12th Dimension was mostly the simple, linear kind. That is, it sparked from the person in charge to the person reporting to the person in charge—from Joe to Ralph or from Ralph to one of his students. It did not go round and round, from one person to the next to the next, and back and forth through the group.

But this Zapp! did.

"So what is it?" asked Joe.

"Gee, I don't know," said Ralph. "It must be because of the teams we read about in *The Horace Mann News*."

"What could be enZapping about teams?" Joe wondered. "We've all tried teams before."

"What I want to know," said Ralph, "is what's making it happen? Cindy is way over there. She isn't even here to do the Zapping!"

That was the other very unusual thing about this type of Zapp! It seemed to have no single source, but instead was generated by the group itself.

Joe watched the wheel of Zapp! and knew that there was more to Zapp! than he understood. Could Zapping people in teams be the next step?

It wouldn't be difficult to set up some faculty and staff teams, Joe reasoned. Even student teams were a possibility. That night, Joe went over the list of teachers and staff at Normal and divided them into teams. The next day, he told everybody at Normal which teams they were on. He even assigned team leaders. Then he asked Ralph to monitor what happened.

A few days later, Ralph came in to announce that the Zapp! count had risen. It was now up to 76 bolts per hour instead of 75.

"Is that all?" asked Joe, obviously disappointed. "OK, Ralph, I'd like your help in finding out why our teams aren't generating more Zapp!"

After some investigating, Ralph determined that the teams were not really teams at all. The Zapp! still flowed from Joe Mode to each team member, rather than around and among the team members in the group.

"You might be calling them teams," said Ralph, "but the teachers and staff members have no more sense of involvement than if they were just a bunch of men and women working in the same building. They're teams in name only."

"Then how come the teams at Zenith Elementary School are enZapping and ours are not?" Joe wondered out loud.

Immediately, the phone rang.

"Because our teams aren't normal work teams," said Cindy Marks when Joe Mode answered the call. "Our teams are Zapped!"

26

"Where are you, Cindy?" asked Joe Mode.

"I'm in the 12th, talking on the Ralphophone. I was just checking up on my own performance, and I could see that you were trying to involve people in teams and not getting very far," Cindy said. "You know, we really should talk more often."

"You're right. We should," agreed Joe.

"I've set up teams, but I'm hardly getting anything for my trouble," continued Joe, obviously discouraged. "What's the secret of your teams?"

"Well," answered Cindy, "we have project teams that take on specific assignments, like the problem we had communicating to students and parents about emergency changes in the school schedule—so we wouldn't have a lot of kids showing up when the school is closed. The project teams function just for specific projects."

"We also have coordinating teams made up of representatives from different areas. They gather and distribute information to help make decisions about their areas of responsibility," she explained.

"But we have those too," said the exasperated Joe.

"Our teams are different," she said. "They're . . . well, for lack of a better term, they're *Zapp! Teams*."

"What do you mean?" asked Joe.

"There are a lot of things that groups of people can do better than individuals working alone," Cindy answered, "because everyone brings unique thoughts, experiences, and information. But the biggest difference is that you can give a team more authority than you can give an individual."

Cindy continued: "Usually you can't give an individual teacher the authority to select new books for a grade level, but you can give a *team* of teachers that responsibility. Teams are a great way of increasing the Zapp! level."

"Aha!" said Joe, who now understood that Zapp! Teams were another extension of the same path his school had been following—which was away from Sapp¡, toward more decision making by those nearest the situation and who needed to have ownership in the decisions.

After he and Cindy hung up, Joe went to work.

First, he asked for help from the teachers in setting up school teams instead of trying to impose *his* set-up on them.

Zapp!

The teams created by the teachers grew out of the basic functions and responsibility areas of Normal Middle School. Once the teams were formed, Joe, as the overall school leader, worked with each team to establish its key result areas.

Joe made sure that everyone understood how each team's key result areas fit in with the overall key result areas of the school and—beyond that—with the overall key result areas of the school district.

Zapp!!

Joe also made sure that the necessary training was available so that all team members would have the knowledge and skills they needed to be successful.

Zapp!!!

From then on, whenever Joe asked for help in solving a big problem, he asked a *team*. When he offered help, he offered help to a *team*.

Zapp!!!!

Day by day, the Zapp! grew within the teams. They came to life. They generated a spirit of their own. And the Zapp! grew within all of Normal Middle School.

Eventually, some of the teams became Super Zapp! Teams.

JOE MODE'S NOTEBOOK

A few things to remember about
Zapp! Teams:

- Creating teams spreads Zapp!
  throughout a school.
- Zapp! Teams are different from
  other kinds of teams.
- A Zapp! Team is more productive
  and creative than a group of Zapped
  individuals.
- The more decisions a team can
  make, the more Zapp! it has.
- To reach super Zapp! levels, a team
  of teachers must be allowed to make
  some of the decisions previously
  made by principals.

27

Each team at Normal Middle School had a leader. The team leader was always someone who was one of the most Zapped in the group, and also one of the most enZapping to others. The leader's role was to coordinate all the things going on in the team and to integrate the team's objectives with the rest of the organization.

Team leader responsibilities usually rotated among members each year so that all the teachers had the opportunity to develop leadership skills.

Joe, of course, remained the overall school leader, as he was now accustomed to thinking of himself.

Sometimes the teachers on a self-directed Zapp! Team could not work things out among themselves, so they would ask Joe for help. But, in time, Joe found that the teams could handle most things on their own most of the time.

In time, the Normal teams chose to work on many new educational and student-related issues. Some of the teams were department specific, like the Language Arts Curriculum Team. Other teams crossed departments, like the Fine Arts Appreciation Team, which included all the art and music teachers, plus other interested teachers from various departments. Joe learned that teams like the Fine Arts Appreciation Team were called *cross-functional* teams.

Some of the teams included students and parents as well as teachers, staff members, and administrators. One of these teams chose to seek out available grants. It also decided to apply for the honor of being named a School of Excellence. "How about that," thought Joe, "from normal to excellent. I like that!"

Another team decided that in order to promote professionalism throughout the school, they would create a Teachers' Center. The team's goal was not only to house the latest professional journals and literature in the center, but to create an environment conducive to professional development. Joe helped here by getting funds for the team from the Central Office. This team had its own budget and was responsible for ordering and purchasing all its own materials.

Another team made up of students, parents, teachers, and staff members was busy preparing for a student to return to school. A few months before, David had been injured in an automobile accident, leaving him a paraplegic. Since the accident, he had been receiving home-bound instruction and had learned to operate a motorized wheelchair. Now he wanted to return to school to be with his friends and classmates. Joe had arranged for extra help for David through special services, but the team wanted to do more.

The teachers on the team decided to spend extra time with David to make sure that he could catch up with his academic work. And because David wanted to participate in extracurricular activities, the parent team members were making plans for his transportation to and from the school during evening hours. The students on the team decided to make sure David got help with his books and personal belongings. Joe practically beamed when he saw how much everyone on the team was looking forward to David's return to Normal.

Another team was made up of special services and regular education teachers who were working on an instructional program for at-risk students. One of the school counselors headed the team, and Joe sometimes observed the team's meetings. Joe was very impressed with the sincerity and dedication of the team members toward helping at-risk students. And he could think of no better leader for this team than the school counselor.

As the team progressed with the at-risk program, parents were invited to attend the meetings and become members. The team knew that the program would be even more successful once it involved the community as well as the school, so it developed an adopt-a-child program that assigned teachers and community members to help certain students.

Joe discovered that in order for teachers and staff to function effectively as members of a team, they needed some new skills. They had to learn new "people" skills—how to interact with one another, how to work things out among themselves when egos and personalities clashed, how to hold effective meetings, and how to solve problems as a group.

No such training programs were available within the district, so with Mary Ellen Krabofski's support, Joe arranged for a local business to share its training programs in these areas. In addition to providing the needed training, this sharing of resources succeeded in bringing the school and an important part of the community closer together.

And, of course, the teams were always introducing new educational and teaching materials. Team members kept abreast of new texts and periodicals on the market and eagerly examined them. Then they would lead discussions at team meetings, sharing what they had learned with other team members.

Joe found that teams also needed new technical skills. He realized this when he requested—and received—federal funding to network the school's computers in classrooms and offices.

A special project team had been created, with members representing all areas of the school, to choose new software that would handle scheduling, grading, attendance, and recording of student information. This system would replace the need for handwritten reports, which would allow the teachers more time to teach.

Early on, the computer coordinator had volunteered to provide in-service training to all the faculty, and Joe had arranged for an all-day training session for this purpose.

At the end of the training session, all the teachers said they understood how to use the software. But as the teachers were added to the network, it became evident that more training was needed. As Joe discovered, giving the same training to all teachers, all at once, without regard for their backgrounds, just didn't work. (And, he realized, if this approach didn't work for teachers, it wouldn't work for students either.)

Teachers who used computers daily as part of their class work or as a personal interest picked up the new program quickly, and were ready to move on. But some teachers dutifully sat through the training session, not understanding one iota about the program, or even knowing how to use a computer. When the time finally rolled around for them to try what they had learned, some didn't know how, and others had forgotten what they were supposed to do.

There was much rolling of eyes and reddening of faces as Joe went about the rather embarrassing job of having to *re*train some of the teachers.

After that, Joe learned to hold off training until a teacher or a team encountered a situation where they really *needed* to learn more—until "the teachable moment." Then teachers would learn more quickly, apply what they learned more effectively, and remember it better.

Joe often had to go to Mary Ellen Krabofski for other resources his teams needed, and Mary Ellen was not always the most receptive boss in the world. Sometimes she would approve his requests with a handshake and a smile, and other times—out of habit—she would give him a cranky and gruff rebuff.

But as Joe Mode's parents used to say, "Where there's a will, there's a way." Because Joe had the will, each time he found a way to get what his teams needed.

As always, Joe kept his notebook up to date.

JOE MODE'S NOTEBOOK

Things that boost the voltage of Zapp! Teams:

- Establish a mission and measurable objectives for the team.
- Provide time and places for the team to meet.
- Provide "people" skills for interacting, holding effective meetings, solving problems, making decisions, and taking action.
- Provide technical training at "the teachable moment."
- Provide ongoing coaching and support.

As they became more confident and better trained, teachers working on the Zapp! Teams began to get involved in making new kinds of decisions. For example, they helped decide who would be on their teams, what texts and teaching materials would be used in their classes, what equipment would be purchased for the school, and what criteria would be used by Principal Joe to evaluate their performance.

Joe continued to learn from the teams and added to his notebook.

JOE MODE'S NOTEBOOK

The more decision making and responsibility, the more Zapp!

Zapp! Teams can handle a lot of responsibility. For instance, they might:

- Determine who teaches what.
- Handle evaluations and performance issues.
- Select their own team leaders from their ranks.
- Find opportunities to improve the quality of instruction.
- Develop Zapped student teams.

The team's responsibilities expanded. But because the responsibilities were shared by the group, every team member had partners to count on.

Not all the new responsibilities were entirely pleasant. For example, it became the team's responsibility to get work done on time and to pull together to solve problems. And if somebody goofed off, then everyone else had to work harder to get the job done or confront the individual.

Most of the teachers didn't like *everything* about teams. But they soon realized that the disadvantages of being on a team were more than offset by what they *liked* about teams.

For instance . . .

They liked having a voice.

They liked agreeing on what to do, rather than being told what to do.

They liked the flexibility of planning their own schedules.

They liked the sense of purpose in having a group mission and being part of the journey to the goal.

They liked being on the inside.

They liked knowing what was going on in the school.

They liked having control over problems.

They liked working with no one looking over their shoulders.

They liked having support from others.

They liked sharing ideas.

They liked sharing the success of the team.

They liked sharing in the power of the team to get things done.

They liked helping the students participate as team members.

All these things were very satisfying. And that was why the Zapp! Teams worked.

JOE MODE'S NOTEBOOK

Why Zapp! Teams work:

1. Communication
2. Creativity
3. Support
4. Flexibility
5. Ownership
6. Sharing
7. **Empowerment**

PART IV

The Zapped School District

28

So, you might ask, what was all this looking like now from the perspective of the wild and wonderful 12th Dimension?

It was dazzling.

Absolutely da-ZZ-ling.

Before the development of Zapp! Teams, each teacher at Normal Middle School had been a glowing island of Zapp! Now the islands were joined, and the flow of Zapp! had become wheels that were revving freely.

Ralph even had to change the scale on the Zappometer to account for Zapp! Teams.

ZAPPOMETER
(bolts per hour)

-100	-50	0	+50	+100	+150

SAPPI   ZAPPI   ZAPP TEAMS!

But seen from the outside . . .

Well, one day Joe, Cindy, and Ralph were outside in the 12th Dimension taking a look at the Normal castles and the effect of the wheels of lightning from the Zapp! Teams.

Indeed, the towers of Normal Middle School and Zenith Elementary School were less castle-like than before. They even appeared to be trying to take off.

"You know," said Joe, "they kind of look like . . . well, like they could go and do just about anything."

"They're like starships, Joe," said Ralph.

"Starships?"

"Sure, ready to take off on a mission."

Well, they may have had the makings of a pair of 12th Dimension starships, but these amazing vehicles were being held on the ground, very securely attached to the gray, heavy mass of the rest of the Normal castle, unable to do all that they were capable of doing.

Somehow, this seemed to be an appropriate *new* challenge—to make the starships fly.

To do it, they would need all the Zapp! they could get. But Ralph (and everyone else as well) had noticed that just when a wheel of Zapp! was turning its fastest and shining its brightest, some source of Sapp¡ would come along to dull it.

Some of these Sapps¡ were BIG ONES.

Big enough even to brake the wheels almost to a stop.

For instance . . .

One morning, Hugh Lancelot (wearing a normal

business suit instead of his 12th Dimension shining armor) walked unexpectedly into Normal Middle School and announced that he and his associates from the Central Office were going to assess the school based on a new set of standards. This process, he explained, was part of a district-wide initiative.

"What makes this evaluation different from the one we had last fall?" asked Cindy Marks.

"We have changed the standards" was the reply. "It's pretty philosophical," Hugh said. "You wouldn't understand. All you need to know is that we have all the answers. We'll take care of everything. We are here to help you."

Sapp¡

"Mr. Lancelot, how can I help?" asked Cindy.

"No need—we will do it all" was the reply. "We will assess your program and write a report on our findings," he explained, holding up an evaluation booklet that was at least three inches thick. "If you want a copy, write to us in three months."

Based on the way Hugh and his crew were acting, Cindy knew that this process would be a Sapp¡ for her school. She tried to explain about the Zapp! Teams and suggested getting the teachers, parents, and students involved. She knew that there were enZapping ways to handle an instructional program assessment, so she pleaded with him to listen. But Hugh Lancelot was set in his ways, and he had his orders from on high. Once he began his work, there was nothing Cindy could do about it.

Hugh Lancelot and his associates treated the teachers objectively. That is, like objects. They hurriedly visited every classroom with their three-inch booklet and said very little to the teachers. They just took note after note.

"What did you think?" asked a teacher proudly, as Hugh and his team started out the door.

"Can't reveal my findings—they're top secret. But I can tell you this. Most of you teachers are not following the recommended lesson-plan procedures. Your students have too much freedom in the classroom. You should be spending more time on teaching and less time on your so-called teams," said Hugh.

Sapp¡¡

And then there was the Central Office. Mary Ellen Krabofski had not had a moment's peace for months.

You see, by now, the mother dragon's eggs were beginning to hatch. And the first thing those baby dragons did was to gorge themselves on anything that could fire up their huffer-puffers.

This actually was not much of a problem for the Zapp! Teams at Normal and Zenith. Against the united Zapp! of a team, the dragons had no chance. By working steadily to improve the quality of instruction and overall teacher and student satisfaction, the Zapp! Teams were giving them no food. So the dragons could not grow.

But in some of the other schools in the district, it was a different story. Some of those baby dragons got very big, very quickly.

Which was why Mary Ellen had had no peace. She was still behind the wheel of the executive fire truck. With all these little fires from the baby dragons breaking out, she was racing here and there, wondering why no one could handle problems as well as she did.

Finally, she had had enough. She went right to Superintendent Browning and pleaded that she desperately needed help with her duties.

After clearing his throat many times, Superintendent Browning reluctantly promised Mary Ellen some assistance. He promised to transfer a person from curriculum to assist her. Which he did.

Outside in the 12th Dimension, a new layer of battlements went up on the castles.

The tallest towers of the castles got even taller, and they got heavier. But the really bad news was that the other towers below got covered up.

One normal afternoon, a parent walked in with a request for Louisa, a first-year counselor at Normal Middle School. "My son, George, is bored in your math and science classes," explained the mother. "He is becoming a behavioral problem in these classes because of this boredom. I've talked to the teachers, and they have given him extra assignments and reports, but it's not helping. I'd like for his schedule to be changed so that he can take high school classes in the afternoon. George thinks he would like that."

Counselor Louisa pulled George's cumulative record and found his grades and test scores to be exceptionally high, especially in math and science. "Gee," said Louisa, who was not quite sure how to handle the situation, "I think that would be great."

Then, Louisa hesitated. She remembered the district's rigid policies. "Well," she said, "first let me check the Rules Manual to see if this action would be appropriate."

Half an hour later, with the parent impatiently squirming in her chair, Louisa announced, "Oh, here's a policy concerning your request. It says that no students can go to high school before their time."

"You're not allowed to place George in more advanced classes even if he needs them?" asked the mother, obviously frustrated.

"I'm not allowed to do that, nor is the principal," said Louisa.

"Then what *can* you do to help George?" demanded the mother.

"Not much," said the young counselor.

Sapp̤ᵢ

Joe Mode was going to the Central Office to see Mary Ellen about some teaching materials he needed at Normal, when he was intercepted by a man in the hallway outside her office.

"Hello, I'm Biff Buffer, the new assistant to the assistant superintendent," he said. "Talk to me when you need anything from now on."

Joe made his request, and Biff said, "Hmmm. I can't give you the go-ahead on something like that right now. You know money is tight. I'll have to clear that with M.E. the next time I see her, and of course I'll have to check with the finance office and the treasurer to see if funds are available. Check back with me in about three or four weeks, and maybe I'll have a decision by then."

"Three or four weeks?" asked Joe, not quite believing his ears.

"Weeks? Did I say *weeks?* Oh, sorry. I meant three or four *months*."

Sapp¡¡¡

All these Sapps¡ coming from forces outside the schools acted like buckets of cold water thrown on the white-hot Zapps! of the faculty and students. It seemed there was little Joe or Cindy or any other principal could do about them.

But then they thought of one thing they could do: They would ask for help from Ralph, who had conducted a study of all the factors that could Zapp! or Sapp¡

This was what Ralph told them he had found:

First, the obvious: The *principal* had the most power to Zapp! or Sapp¡ the *teachers* and *staff members* in the school.

The *teachers* had the most power to Zapp! or Sapp¡ the *students* in the school.

And the *students* had the most power to Zapp! or Sapp¡ the *parents* of the school.

However, Ralph had found that a lot of other things affected Zapp! levels—and most were products of the Central Administration. The district's policies and regulations took away school ownership, control, and decision making.

"Joe, the plain truth is that there are lots of things affecting Sapp¡ and Zapp! that we can't control," said Cindy.

"Well, we're still better off than we were," decided Joe. "My life is easier. I'm not about to go back to Sapping people. Everybody in the school is happier now."

"True, but I'm not satisfied with that," said Cindy. "I think it's time to talk to Mary Ellen."

"I agree," said Joe. "But first, let me make some notes in my notebook about the ideas we came up with."

JOE MODE'S NOTEBOOK

Who determines how Zapped (or Sapped) a teacher is?

In order of importance:

1. The teacher's immediate principal (the school leader).
2. The other people who affect the teacher's job within the school (other teachers, service and support personnel).
3. Central Office administrators.
4. The district's policies and regulations.

By far, the teacher's most important enZapping influence is the principal.

JOE MODE'S NOTEBOOK

Policies and regulations have the power to Zapp! and Sappi too:

- Compensation
- Communication
- Appraisal/Evaluation
- Personnel policies
- Discipline
- Selection and promotion
- Information
- Training and development
- Travel reimbursement
- Career planning
- Suggestion system

29

Though she could be quite trollish from time to time, Mary Ellen Krabofski was no dummy. In fact, she was very smart. She soon began to notice that she had to spend very little time solving problems for Normal Middle or Zenith Elementary schools.

Of course, she knew about some amazing things going on in those schools, such as the awards Zenith had won, and she especially wanted to know why Normal Middle School, where performance had always been mediocre at best, was now so great.

In fact, word was spreading quickly throughout Normal School District. Lots of teachers wanted to transfer into the two schools because both had earned the reputation of being wonderful places to teach. Even some of the other principals had begun to ask what was going so *right* at Normal and Zenith.

About then, Joe and Cindy came to a conclusion: It was time to take the wraps off, time to go public. They had done in their own schools as much as they could with Zapp! To go further, they needed the help of the entire school system.

So Joe and Cindy went to their Zapp! Teams and asked for their help in developing a presentation for the superintendent and the Board of Education. The teams went right to work.

First, they asked some students and parents to be part of the presentation. Then they set up a meeting date with Superintendent Browning, who was quite receptive to hearing what they had to say. As the big evening approached, Joe and Cindy coached the Zapp! Team presenters on what to expect, what would be expected of them, and how to make a successful presentation.

When the big evening arrived, Joe opened the presentation. He began by giving a glowing description of the power of Zapp! and how fantastic it was. Of course, no superlative for Zapp! was too great. Everyone was impressed.

Then he said, "Mary Ellen, we've wired your chair to the Ralpholator. We're going to turn it on now, and in a moment you'll be whisked to the 12th Dimension where you'll see the wonders of Zapp! at work right before your very eyes."

Joe turned to the back of the room and said, "OK, Ralph, hit it."

There was a high-pitched whine. Followed by a low-pitched whine. And then *nothing* happened.

"Excuse me. We seem to have some technical difficulties," muttered Joe.

With a reddened face, Ralph stood up in the rear

of the room and said quietly, "Bad news, Joe, the Ralpholator is broken. It blew its hootennannies."

Joe turned and looked at Mary Ellen.

The somewhat cross-eyed expression on her face said it all: She was embarrassed.

Lightning, huh? Human lightning, you say? Yeah, right. *Wheels* of lightning, no less. Sure. Was there a *truck* attached to the wheels? Did you happen to get its license number?

Who could believe such nonsense?

Well, Joe made a very quick—and wise—decision. He continued with the presentation. The Zapp! Teams came up one by one. The teachers talked about their teaching and about being Zapped. They talked about quality teaching, helping students, enhanced learning, and higher test scores. The students talked about how much they enjoyed school, how much they were learning, and how well they were treated. The parents explained how much they all appreciated Normal and Zenith, because their kids liked school and were doing well.

All these comments were magical music to the superintendent's and the board members' ears.

And the *way* the Zapp! Team members talked demonstrated that Normal and Zenith teachers could take responsibility for their work on an everyday basis to a degree that people like Mary Ellen never would have thought possible.

As it turned out, they didn't need the Ralpholator or the 12th Dimension to convince the superintendent and the board members. And best of all, Mary Ellen Krabofski was impressed. By the end of the presentation, she was positively Zapped!

Most of all, she wanted her other schools to be Zapped the same way—right away.

"We have to tell everyone about this!" exclaimed Mary Ellen. She was very excited. "I want every principal to have teams—uh, what are you calling them? Zapp! Teams? That's it, *Zapp! Teams!* I want all our schools to start using Zapp! ASAP!"

No one is more dedicated to a cause than a skeptic who becomes convinced.

Mary Ellen scheduled a meeting of all the principals, attempting to convince them that Zapp! was the way for everybody to go.

This didn't work.

The other principals nodded their heads, agreed that Zapp! made sense, and then went back to being the same kind of principals they had always been.

But from this, Mary Ellen learned something important: To create Zapp!, she had to use Zapp!

The other schools had to discover Zapp! on their own. With her enZapping help, of course.

She began with the first three principles of Zapp!

1. **Maintain self-esteem.**
2. **Listen and respond with empathy.**
3. **Ask for help and encourage involvement.**

Mary Ellen began practicing these principles in all her dealings with the principals and teachers. And, of course, she found that the principles were as applicable to her as they were to Joe, Cindy, or anyone else in a leadership role.

Then she applied the soul of Zapp!:

Offer help without
taking responsibility for action.

One day, the police department called Mary Ellen about a drug problem at Typical High School. Normally, Mary Ellen would have headed up an investigation and taken personal charge. But this time she asked the principal what should be done and then offered her help in implementing the plan. She coached and added input from her own experience, but the problem and the solution clearly remained with the school.

As the assistant superintendent, Mary Ellen realized that she had an essential role to play: to support the kind of environment where Zapp! could develop and flourish.

For instance, she encouraged all the principals to get formal training in Zapp!, and she made available the resources for this training to take place.

Then, just as Joe had done for Normal, Mary Ellen asked all the other schools' principals to develop performance guidelines with key result areas, measurements, and goals.

But one of the most important things Mary Ellen realized she had to do was to protect people from the Sapping things that the superintendent or the school board might attempt to do, while encouraging Zapping from above.

To be quite honest, it took Mary Ellen a long time to relinquish the keys to the executive fire truck. It wasn't easy. But as she continued to apply Zapp!, a change came over her.

In fact, when Joe took his occasional walks around the 12th Dimension, he hardly recognized Mary Ellen. Her color was no longer ghastly green. Her scales had melted. Her tail grew shorter, and then it disappeared. Soon, she was no longer a troll. Zapp! had changed her into a human being, the true form of all good school administrators.

When Joe talked with Mary Ellen about the changes, she told him what she had learned. And Joe made sure he wrote everything down so that he wouldn't forget.

JOE MODE'S NOTEBOOK

The Central Office's role in spreading Zapp!:

1. To protect teachers from the Sapping things the district might attempt to do, while supporting and encouraging the Zapping things the district can offer.
2. To be sure that principals and team leaders have the skills required to Zapp! (And if they don't, get them into training.)
3. To coach principals and teachers on how to use and improve their Zapp! skills.
4. To reward performance resulting from Zapp!

Overall: to create an environment where Zapp! can happen.

30

Now you'd think that training in Zapp! skills—in other words, *education*—would be a natural for a school district. But alas, it was not to be that easy. First, the teachers and principals were placed into classes where they heard lectures about Zapp! People didn't change much.

Next, Mary Ellen tried role playing. Selected trainees were called to the front of the room and asked to imagine that they were in a difficult situation where they had the opportunity to use Zapp! and then demonstrate what they would do. Most would fail, and then their failures would be discussed by the class, as the instructor made learning points based on everyone's mistakes.

Few skills were learned, because only a few people actually got to practice. And the roleplayers lost confidence in themselves because of their failure experiences. Seeing what had happened to the roleplayers, the rest of the class realized that they would also find it difficult if placed in a similar situation in real life, and their confidence went down too.

Then, there was the problem of time. Everyone thought skills training was a good idea, but nobody wanted to spend the time to do it.

Several principals attended an outside course, where they spent three days learning Zapp! skills. Based on their glowing report, the administration decided to hold an in-house program in the district. However, only one day was allowed for what had been covered by the experts in three days. It didn't have the same impact.

Observing all this, Joe got out his notebook and wrote down some of what he'd learned about behavioral skills training.

JOE MODE'S NOTEBOOK

Behavioral Skills Training:

1. It's hard to preach people into changing their behavior.
2. Developing confidence is just as important as developing skills.
3. Changing behavior takes time. There is no substitute for practice with feedback. Watching someone else practice doesn't do it.

Much to its credit, the district continued to experiment. After one particularly frustrating training experience, one of the coaches from the high school made the comment, "It looks to me like these Zapp! principles are skills, just like passing or catching a ball. When we get a bunch of new recruits, we talk to them about what needs to be done, we demonstrate it, we let them practice, and then we tell them how they are doing. In other words, we *coach* them. Why couldn't we do the same thing in a training program?"

"Oh, no. We couldn't do that. That means that the groups would be too small," said an administrator. "Imagine how much it would cost to give everybody an opportunity to practice skills in every training program."

But after much discussion, they settled the issue with a telling insight: *Any money spent on training that doesn't work is wasted. No matter how cheap or short the training is.*

Changing from a lecture format was a difficult transition for the administration and the teachers. Most of their past training had involved lecture/discussion formats, with a few case studies or other exercises thrown in. Anything else seemed strange.

After a little investigation, though, Mary Ellen found that the technology they were exploring had a name: *behavior modeling*. And a great deal of research had been done about its effectiveness in developing people's skills and confidence.

Mary Ellen shared this information with all the principals, and that's how it got into Joe's notebook.

JOE MODE'S NOTEBOOK

Behavior Modeling Steps:

1. Discuss the importance and relevance of the skill to be learned.
2. Discuss the principles or steps important to becoming successful in the skill.
3. Demonstrate the principles or steps. (Consider using videotape.)
4. Allow all participants an opportunity to practice the new skill and to receive feedback.
5. Coach participants prior to their practice opportunity to ensure success.
6. Train the participants who are observing the skill practice session to give supportive, balanced feedback.

NOTEBOOK (cont'd)

7. Before they leave the training session, encourage the participants to commit to specific on-the-job applications.

Behavior modeling is a classroom application of coaching.

Supervisors need to be trained in the same skills as participants, and they need to know how to coach and reinforce the participants' on-the-job behavior.

At least five skill practice sessions are necessary for the average participant to develop skills and confidence in using the Zapp! key principles.

Joe learned from Mary Ellen that the thing that made behavior modeling training in Zapp! skills effective was that after people had the opportunity to try out skills in the nurturing environment of a training room, they had the confidence to try out the skills on the job.

The success they obtained and the supportive reinforcement from their supervisors and peers created even more confidence. So they kept practicing, becoming more skilled and confident.

It wasn't easy, and it certainly didn't work all the time. But behavior modeling got the skill deficit turned around, and that's what everyone wanted.

31

Biff Buffer was as nervous as a 40-year-old quarterback holding out for a fatter contract on the day the final cuts are made.

As the assistant to the assistant superintendent, Biff knew that his job security was not a sure thing anymore because of all the changes taking place throughout the district. He worried about all this Zapp! stuff.

In cases where layers and layers of administrators had been stripped away, there had been a big increase in Zapp! That made Biff nervous.

When Superintendent Browning called Biff into his office one Friday to meet with him and Mary Ellen Krabofski, Biff imagined that he heard the upswing of the ax. But the superintendent had something much smarter in mind.

"Biff, you're an intelligent and capable administrator. It's the nature of your position that's the issue, not your professional performance," said Superintendent Browning, attempting to maintain Biff's self-esteem.

"Well, I can always try to work harder and be

much more efficient, if you'll just give me the chance," said Biff.

"I sense that you're nervous about your job, and I'd like to put your mind at ease," said Superintendent Browning, responding with empathy after having listened to what Biff had (and had not) said.

Then Superintendent Browning asked for help in solving a problem, saying, "I'd like your help in an important undertaking. If we are to reach new educational horizons, we must have involvement at every level—students, teachers, support staff, principals, the Central Office, parents, and the entire community. With the advance of Zapp! in our schools, we are getting more and more good recommendations for improvement, but nothing is happening to make these recommendations a reality. I know it's causing frustration. Something is wrong, and I'd like your help."

The superintendent then discussed with Biff what he might need for a team to get to the bottom of the problem and assured Biff that he would have whatever support was needed. He wanted to meet periodically with Mary Ellen and Biff to discuss the progress of the team and to explain any difficulties encountered, so they scheduled some progress meetings.

"You'll be in charge," said Superintendent Browning to Biff, "but Mary Ellen will continue to work with you." With this, Mary Ellen Krabofski smiled and nodded her consent to this new plan.

Biff sat upright in his chair. He was feeling the call of a new challenge and the excitement of working to meet it. As the meeting ended, he was on Cloud Nine.

Later in the day, Mary Ellen gave Biff some general directions about organizing a Zapp! Team and outlined some of the challenges he might encounter.

Then she said, "I'd like for us to meet again after you've had time to put together some ideas," thus offering to help without taking responsibility. "And be sure to talk to me whenever you need my help or extra resources to get this done."

Zapp!

Biff Buffer caught the lightning that Superintendent Browning and Mary Ellen Krabofski had thrown him, and he ran with it.

Within a month, Biff had formulated a Zapp! Team, including in its membership representatives of all the groups the superintendent had requested. Then Biff went one step further and included a board member. Immediately the Zapp! Team went to work on ways to encourage the *application* of innovation.

The Zapp! Team members sought ways to stimulate initiative. Instead of "snoopervising" and creating rules to try to control everybody, they started looking for ways that the Central Office could minimize control over teachers and principals and help them bring out the best in themselves and their students.

All this made the Board of Education and the superintendent (and everybody else) a lot happier, and it made the Normal School District a better place to be.

JOE MODE'S NOTEBOOK

- School teams can create Zapp!
- Central Office teams can create Zapp!

32

By now, Zenith Elementary School had gained recognition not only in the schools but also with parents and the community. More and more parents were requesting, and being given permission, to transfer their children into Zenith. For some reason, this was happening a lot at the second-grade level. In fact, the work load for the second-grade teachers had grown so much that they couldn't possibly do everything they needed to do with such large classes. Quite simply, the school needed another second-grade teacher.

As she was obligated to do by Normal district policy, Cindy went to the personnel department with the proper authorization from Mary Ellen, and personnel approved her hiring request.

A while later, Nathaniel showed up. A recent college graduate, this was his first job. "They sent me over. Guess I'm your new second-grade teacher," said Nathaniel.

Cindy introduced him to the Zenith staff. And the teachers took an instant dislike to Nathaniel.

It wasn't that there was anything *wrong* with Nathaniel. He was not a fugitive from justice or wanted by the FBI, and he had all the proper teaching credentials for the position. But nobody could get very excited about having Nathaniel on the Zenith team.

Why should they? No one on the Zenith staff had been involved in selecting Nathaniel. Nothing was personally at stake for any of them if Nathaniel didn't work out.

Not even Cindy Marks had a stake in Nathaniel's success. No one in the personnel department had even asked her about the special requirements for a second-grade teacher at her school.

And Nathaniel was not very excited about his first assignment either. Zenith School? Big deal. *They* hadn't selected him. The *personnel director* had selected him.

Nathaniel was Sapped for a long time.

Cindy realized this, and the next time Zenith needed a new teacher, she asked Mary Ellen to talk to the personnel department about modifying the procedures in order to make them more enZapping.

Mary Ellen gladly presented the situation to the personnel director and asked for her help in working with Cindy and the other principals.

And this time, the results were very different.

Not only did the team interview the candidates, but it also devised creative ways to evaluate how well the candidates would fit into a Zapped organization. For example, candidates were given a standardized description about a young boy with learning and behavior problems. After time to prepare, each candidate conducted a simulated meeting with the boy's "mother" (played by a team member).

The team evaluated classroom skills by asking each candidate to prepare and present a lesson to a class of students at the grade level the new teacher would be teaching. It prepared special observation forms so that every candidate would be evaluated according to the same criteria.

After much discussion of strengths and weaknesses compared to a list of predetermined required skills it had devised, the team made a decision. It was a big Zapp! for everyone.

It was a Zapp! for the personnel director: She could see that the school was getting a teacher who would be effective and comfortable in a Zapped environment.

It was a Zapp! for the school staff because the teachers had had a say in who would work with them. Taking part in the selection decision gave the teachers ownership in the selected individual's success. They naturally took on responsibility for the individual's development and willingly did everything they could to ensure that the chosen teacher would be successful.

Involving teachers in the selection process also helped to develop their teaching skills. The act of setting up and running the selection process had helped all involved become better teachers, because it caused them to focus on the specific behaviors really important to being a successful teacher at Zenith Elementary School.

Not surprisingly, it was a huge Zapp! for the new teacher to be chosen by the principal and school team instead of being imposed upon them. In fact, the new teacher worked even harder than usual to keep from disappointing Cindy or the school.

Meanwhile, over at Normal Middle School, things were beginning to change too. The teachers and counselors were interested not only in having more say about what direction Normal Middle School was going, but also in dealing with the parents to promote understanding and acceptance of the new concepts. Believe it or not, Normal counselors and teachers actually began to look forward to meeting with angry parents because they wanted the opportunity to explain things and watch dissatisfaction turn to satisfaction.

One afternoon, for instance, a determined parent stomped into Normal and yelled, "I demand to talk to the principal! This stupid idea of forcing fine arts on everyone is a joke. No kid of mine is going to take 'Music Appreciation.' You should be teaching the three Rs around here."

Joe was off in the 12th Dimension, but the counselor heard the parent's complaint and invited him into her office for a visit. Reluctantly, the parent accepted the offer.

As the meeting began, the counselor said, "You're right, Mr. Martin. We should, and we are, teaching the three Rs at Normal. But we do it in different ways."

"But what about this fine arts program for my Sam?" interrupted Mr. Martin.

"I know exactly how you feel. You're concerned that Sam gets a good grounding in the basics to prepare him for the rest of school—and life. That's what every good parent wants," said the counselor. "Here's what I'll do. Let me explain what I know about the new program and answer any questions you might have. Then we'll visit a couple of classrooms to let you see the program in action. We can talk with the teachers about it too."

Mr. Martin agreed.

After talking with the counselor, and after visiting and talking with two teachers, Mr. Martin understood the new program. And he liked it! He wanted his son to continue in the program. As he left the building, Mr. Martin actually smiled.

Zapp!

In the meantime, Biff Buffer's team was accomplishing a lot in the area of encouraging continuous improvement applications. Everyone agreed that good ideas were valuable only when they were implemented.

The big problem seemed to be the conflict between the need for independent decision making by the teachers and staff, and the need for coordination within and among schools. In other words, every teacher or team of teachers couldn't be allowed to do his or her own thing because this would mean utter chaos. And there were important questions to be answered: How could year-to-year continuity be developed? What if students transferred to other schools?

Biff's team thought hard.

They figured out something very important: Because many people are affected by a teacher's or a team's decisions, the needs of all these *stakeholders* must be considered in the decision-making process. Obviously, the greater people's involvement, the greater the chance for a good decision and a successful *implementation*.

Finally, it became clear that Zapp! did not mean independence; it meant *inter*dependence.

But how would they get teachers to accept this idea? Many of the teachers were acting like teenagers reacting to a new-found adult freedom—wanting to be totally independent, after years of childhood dependence. They wanted to do their own thing. Few even thought they needed training—until they experienced their first failures.

As teachers stretched the limits of their freedom and started to make changes, many found that they weren't getting the cooperation or resources that they needed to implement their ideas. "It's the bureaucracy" was a frequent lament.

Others found that what seemed like a good idea initially proved—after a lot of work to implement it—not to be such a good idea after all. Because they had the opportunity to commit themselves and take action, even failure was a Zapp! But succeeding would be a much bigger Zapp! How could a teacher's batting average be improved?

It was the revelation that they couldn't do things alone that got the teachers into training. And Biff's team responded with a program that combined problem-solving skills with involvement techniques. The team offered teachers and principals a six-step approach to problem solving.

At each step, the teachers were taught to identify stakeholders and to determine the most appropriate ways to involve these people. They learned that having a lot of different views can help improve ideas. "After all," Joe reminded them, "two heads are better than one."

The teachers also learned that a lot of ideas had been tried before, with varying degrees of success, and that a quick trip to the library to check the professional literature saved a great deal of time and effort.

Principals, teachers, and support staff all attended the program. And that's how the problem-solving steps made it into Joe Mode's Notebook.

JOE MODE'S NOTEBOOK

Problem-solving Steps:

1. Assess improvement opportunities.
2. Determine causes.
3. Target solutions and ideas.
4. Implement actions.
5. Evaluate effectiveness.
6. Make it ongoing.
   * Document.
   * Standardize.

33

Not only was the district encouraging continuous improvement ideas within each classroom, they were also encouraging system-wide ideas.

As you might have expected, Ralph Rosco was one of the first to come up with a good idea.

Ralph thought, *"Gee, I wonder if they'd be interested in my Ralpholator as a new teaching device?"*

So he went to Joe and reminded him of his promise long ago to help develop Ralph's invention. True to his word, Joe did help, and he cleared the way for Ralph to talk to the assistant superintendent that afternoon after school.

Unfortunately, in this case Mary Ellen Krabofski reacted out of old habit. After hearing Ralph's presentation, she told Ralph to submit his idea in writing and she'd suggest it to the Central Office administrators. If the Central Office people liked the idea, they'd let Ralph know. And if they didn't like it, they'd let Ralph know that too.

Ralph went back to his classroom, dusted off his Normal employee handbook, and turned to the page that explained the Normal system for getting Central Office approval for new ideas.

According to the handbook, Ralph was supposed to get somebody in the Central Office to submit his idea at a staff meeting. That much, he'd done. It was on its way.

Next, Ralph was supposed to do nothing. Except wait for the verdict.

In a few months, the powers-that-be would pass judgment. If *they* thought the idea might be worthwhile for Normal, they would notify Ralph.

From experience, Ralph could tell this was a very Sappy system. After submitting the idea, Ralph would be completely uninvolved. The Central Office would own his Ralpholator idea.

Because Ralph felt he would be excluded from the evaluation process, he suspected that no matter what was said, the idea probably would not be communicated as effectively as he could have done it. After all, it was *his* idea.

So Ralph explained this to Joe and said, "There has to be a better way."

Joe encouraged Ralph to take responsibility for the consequences (whether good or bad) of what he was suggesting. Then he helped Ralph examine his idea in a practical context.

"Your Ralpholator is a neat machine, but how is the district going to use it?" Joe asked.

Well, Ralph hadn't thought about that. "Gee, I don't know. But it must have a *zillion* applications."

"Name two," said Joe.

Ralph couldn't.

"Why don't you work on that a little more, and then we'll talk again," suggested Joe.

So Ralph did some more thinking.

He decided that one use for the Ralpholator might be in the counseling department. The counselors and school psychologists who talked with students about their problems could go to the 12th Dimension and see for themselves exactly how the students reacted to what was happening.

Even more important, Ralph reasoned, the faculty could use it to evaluate themselves. Teachers could see what was happening in their classrooms and then determine if their continuous improvement ideas were effective.

Were the students really learning? Were they having fun learning?

"But how can teachers see themselves?" asked Joe. "How can they be in the real world and the 12th Dimension at the same time?"

"Good question, Joe," answered Ralph. "My newest idea—and maybe the best idea of all—is to tweak the Ralpholator so that teachers can tape their classes and then watch themselves later . . . sort of like taping a TV show with your VCR. I haven't worked out all the bugs yet, but I'm sure I can."

This would be the Ralpholator's main selling point, Ralph decided: self-evaluation and self-improvement.

"That's good," said Joe when Ralph outlined the machine's potential at their next meeting. "I'll give you the names of a couple of art teachers who are great with visuals. Maybe you can get them to help you develop visual aids to use when you present your plan."

The visuals were developed. In fact, the art teachers liked playing a role in this important project and gladly volunteered their time.

Next, Joe helped Ralph to see that the Ralpholator controls were not as user friendly as they might be. There was a chance that people who were uncomfortable with computers might send themselves off in the wrong dimension. Ralph fixed that problem.

Then Ralph went to the district's purchasing director to get help in developing some cost estimates.

Finally, Joe gave Ralph some basic training on how to make a formal presentation. Then he arranged for Ralph to present his ideas to the assistant superintendent.

When Ralph appeared before Mary Ellen Krabofski, he was ready. He had a lot more than just a neat machine to show her. He had visuals, a cost analysis, and, more important, ideas for improving instruction in the Normal School District.

Mary Ellen was so impressed that she asked Ralph to make the same presentation to Superintendent Browning and the Board of Education at their next meeting.

And that was how the Ralpholator got on the road to success. Joe had helped and guided Ralph. But it had been Ralph's idea, and he felt the all-important surge of pride when the idea was accepted. Joe realized that this was another successful application of *offering help without taking responsibility for action*.

34

Years passed.

One morning, Joe Mode was working in his office when Phyllis knocked on his door and said, "Excuse me, Joe, but there's a young man out here who says he'd like to ask you some questions about how we run Normal Middle School."

Joe asked Phyllis to send him in.

"What's your name?" Joe asked the young man, as he sat down.

"I'm Rick," said the young man.

"Well, Rick, what can I do for you?"

"I'm the new assistant principal at the high school, and Mary Ellen Krabofski sent me over to your school to learn about something called Zapp! I understand your school was one of the first to start using it," said Rick.

"That's true," said Joe proudly.

"I've heard Zapp! is the energy that enables continuous improvement."

"That's also true," said Joe.

"Well, how does it work?" asked Rick.

By now, Joe was quite accustomed to inquiries by the curious. He'd been explaining Zapp! to school principals and teachers for years. And it seemed that every month, he had something new to report.

It was important, he'd explain to everyone, to remember that Zapp! is a gradual process. It doesn't happen all at once.

Joe took Rick for a tour, showing him Normal Middle School and introducing him to some of the Zapp! Teams, whose teachers gladly explained what they did and how they worked together. Most of the teachers were careful to point out that learning about Zapp! took a lot of time and energy. It wasn't an easy process. But the results were worth it.

At the end of the tour, Joe took Rick to the 12th Dimension so that he could see Zapp! in living color. Finally, to give Rick the "big picture," Joe showed him a new feature of the 12th Dimension: It was a big, round observation deck that afforded a magnificent view of the Normal School District and the many school districts surrounding it.

From horizon to horizon, through the gaps in the drifting mists and fog, they could see all kinds of school castles scattered about the countryside.

Over here, on a rocky rise, was a typical, large castle, which looked much like the Normal castle had years ago, with sentries posted and lots of people coming and going through its gates.

And over there was a crumbling, dark, deserted castle sinking into a swamp.

Off on the horizon was Abnormal School District, a huge, high, and impossibly complex castle with towers reaching into the clouds—into and *above* the clouds, in fact. Its top administrators probably couldn't even see the ground from up there. With its miles of maze-like walls and moats, it looked like nothing could ever topple Abnormal, that it would stand forever.

But just then, gliding among the tallest towers, Joe and Rick saw *flying* dragons. As they watched, one of the dragons, clinging to the sides of one of the biggest towers, munched its way through the walls—chomp, chomp, chomp—until the tower fell over like an axed tree and landed with an enormous crash. Indeed, for all its size and grim complexity, the Abnormal castle seemed hopelessly antiquated compared with the shape of their own Normal School District.

In fact, most of Normal these days did not even look like castles. Normal School District looked more like a launching pad, a home base for people who took off every morning in a wide-ranging fleet of amazing craft that had been designed with the help of those who flew them. The fleet was propelled by the energy of Zapp!

As Joe and Rick looked around, they could see all the Normal teachers out there in the wild blue, flying their missions, getting their jobs done. And best of all, the Normal students were piloting their own space crafts—many with fantastic shapes they had designed themselves.

Of course, in reality, everybody was down here on

Planet Earth in good old America. But to every Normal staff member, it felt *good* to go to work. Their ordinary jobs were far from ordinary anymore.

"Looks like we're way ahead of lots of other districts out there," said Rick.

"Yes, we are. And we're pulling away," Joe said.

"But don't we ever have trouble with dragons here?" asked Rick.

"Sure, we still have a few, and every once in a while a new one will hatch," admitted Joe. "Dragons are tough and some of them nearly immortal. But as our teachers keep getting better and better, our dragons keep getting smaller and smaller. They have less and less to feed on, as we keep improving."

Joe pointed out to Rick that he should not get the idea that the transformation of Normal was finished or ever would be. Zapp! was not fixed or absolute, he explained, but a driving force for a journey toward continuous improvement. Sometimes the road was rough, and sometimes they even slid backwards. But by working together—Zapping together—they were making real progress.

Off to the sides, many parts of the old castle were still being remodeled, recycled into flightworthy *Zapp-craft*. Even the craft now flying undoubtedly would evolve into new forms as time went on. And over on the next hill was the landing base for a whole new 12th Dimension fleet—the Ultranormal Fleet—that was expanding into new educational horizons.

That new fleet, by the way, was commanded by

none other than Biff Buffer, and it was managed and operated by many of those individuals who otherwise would have been squeezed in the flattening of the Normal School District. Now they were off the ground and Zapped on missions of their own. And Ralph was flying with them.

The Ralpholator had become as important to Normal as the computer. At the request of the superintendent, Ralph was no longer teaching full time. He spent part of each day working with his district team to keep improving the Ralpholator. In his new role, Ralph not only kept in touch with Joe on a regular basis, but he had the satisfaction of helping the teachers and principals in *all* the schools in the district.

All this had taken a long time, Joe explained. It had not been easy, but it certainly had been worth it. Not only did teachers come to work excited about teaching, but students came to school eager to learn.

As they started back, Rick asked, "Zapp! is something I can use in my own job . . . but what do I do first?"

Joe was ready for this question because in the years since he and Ralph had first learned about Zapp! from Cindy Marks, lots of people had asked him how they might generate some human lightning of their own.

"Allow me to recommend my Three-step Action Plan for Zapp! Rookies," said Joe. "Let's go back to my office, and I'll get you started."

The first thing Joe did when they got back from the 12th Dimension was to give Rick a copy of the Joe

Mode Notebook so that he could study the basic principles of Zapp!

"Here, read this. Start with Step One. I even reread the notebook myself every so often to refresh my memory," said Joe.

"OK, but is reading this going to be enough?" Rick asked.

"Probably not," said Joe. "That's why I suggest you try Step Two. Come with me."

He took Rick to the Central Office to meet the district's staff development director, Cindy Marks.

"Rick, meet Cindy," said Joe. "She's now the district's voice for Zapp!"

"Pleased to meet you, Rick," said Cindy. "Are you here to get some Zapp! training?"

"Gee, I don't know. Do I really need training?" asked Rick.

"Well, you could learn the skills to improve Zapp! by trial and error, the way I did," said Joe. "But that takes a long time, and you can make a lot of unnecessary mistakes. What I recommend is that you build your basic skills in Cindy's training programs so that you're more likely to succeed with Zapp! the first time you try."

Rick considered that idea. "Yes, that does sound more efficient."

"And it'll be easier on the old anxiety level," added Joe, smiling.

With that, Rick signed up for Cindy's introductory program.

Then as he and Joe were leaving, Rick asked, "And what's the third step in your Three-step Action Plan for Zapp! Rookies?"

"Don't stop," said Joe.

"What do you mean by that?"

"I mean, once you're on the right path, keep trying, keep learning, keep improving, keep growing," said Joe. "In short, don't stop. Keep learning."

"Well, OK. I'll give it my best," said Rick.

"Good. And if I can be of any more help to you, let me know," offered Joe.

"Thanks," said Rick as they shook hands.

As Rick walked away, Joe could almost see the Zapp! beginning to grow inside a new assistant principal. And that made him happy because he knew that once Rick saw the power of Zapp!, he'd share it with his teachers. And once the teachers saw the power of Zapp!, they'd share it with their students.

Joe Mode smiled as he realized that that's what Ralph had been trying to tell him years ago when he first invented the Ralpholator. Teaching and learning could be exciting. Zapp! could be exciting!

Joe glanced down at his well-worn notebook.

JOE MODE'S NOTEBOOK

Three-step Action Plan for Zapp!
Rookies:

1. Read (and reread) the notebook!
2. Get training in Zapp!
3. Don't stop! Keep learning!

As Joe turned to walk back to his office, he saw two high school students waiting for him down the hallway. Immediately, he recognized Sophie and Benjamin. Sophie was smiling and Benjamin was grinning from ear to ear.

"Hi, Mr. Mode!" they both shouted.

"Well, it's Benjamin and Sophie, two of my favorite students. Congratulations on your high school graduation next month. I'm quite proud of both of you," Joe said. "What's the occasion for this visit?"

"Well," said Sophie, "we have something to tell you."

"Yes," said Benjamin. "We've both been accepted at State Teachers College."

"In fact," Sophie joined in, "we've been awarded scholarships, and we plan to be teachers—just like the teachers at Normal."

Joe smiled. He wondered if the two students still remembered that first bolt of lightning in the 12th Dimension. He knew that *he* would never forget it.

ACKNOWLEDGMENTS

The best-selling book *Zapp! The Lightning of Empowerment* was written with the substantial collaboration of Jeff Cox, who was responsible for most of the imaginative presentations of concepts. I also had valuable collaboration in producing *Zapp! in Education*.

Kathy Shomo, the manager of Publishing Services at Development Dimensions International (DDI), managed the project and wrote several sections. Kathy's project management included sending manuscript drafts to leading educators throughout the United States and incorporating their excellent feedback. These reviewers included:

- John Cullen, Supervisor, Wayne County Schools Career Center, Ohio

- Alan Ellis, President, Learning Solutions, Florida

- David Kimmelman, Principal, Marie G. Davis School, North Carolina

- Dale Lumley, English Department Chairperson, Butler Area School District, Pennsylvania

- Gerard Mack, Principal, Jarrettsville Elementary School, Maryland

- Bob Millward, Assessment Director, Indiana University of Pennsylvania

- Luther R. Rogers, Chief, Florida Department of Education

Many associates from DDI also made important contributions by critiquing various drafts, offering ideas, and providing real-life examples from their personal experiences; others worked diligently on the production of the book. Individuals who deserve special recognition include Linda Appel, Andrea Eger, Shelby Gracey, Anne Maers, Carol Schuetz, Miriam Vandale, and Ellen Wellins. Other DDI associates who assisted with *Zapp! in Education* include Tammy Bercosky, Linda Kapustynski, Dyan Moorhead, and Dee Weaver. Special thanks to Stacy Rae Zappi and Pamela A. Miller for the book's cover design, and Tom Cwenar for the cover photography.

Development Dimensions International (DDI) offers numerous training programs to give school leaders the skills necessary to make empowerment a reality in their schools. DDI also provides seminars and presentations to show how Zapp! can be an integral part of a school's daily operations. For more information about DDI's products and services, call the Zapp! hotline at (412) 257-2277.

Now that you have read *Zapp! in Education,* we encourage you to share your thoughts on the book and its application in your schools. Write to us at Development Dimensions International, World Headquarters—Pittsburgh, 1225 Washington Pike, Bridgeville, PA 15017-2838.